OUR DESIRE OF UNREST

OUR DESIRE OF UNREST
Thinking about Therapy

Michael Jacobs

KARNAC

First published in 2009 by
Karnac Books Ltd
118 Finchley Road, London NW3 5HT

British Library Cataloguing in Publication Data

A C.I.P. for this book is available from the British Library

ISBN: 978 1 85575 489 8

Edited, designed and produced by The Studio Publishing Services Ltd,
www.publishingservicesuk.co.uk
e-mail: studio@publishingservicesuk.co.uk

www.karnacbooks.com

kind permission of Taylor and Francis. The Journal's website is http://www.informaworld.com.

Chapter Seven first appeared in the *European Journal of Psychotherapy, Counselling and Health*, 1998, 1(2): 213–230, and is reproduced with the kind permission of Taylor and Francis. The Journal's website is http://www.informaworld.com.

Chapter Eight was published as a monograph in 1994 by the Clinical Theology Association, which has since changed its name to the Bridge Pastoral Foundation. The slightly abridged version in this chapter is reproduced with the kind permission of the Bridge Pastoral Association.

ACKNOWLEDGEMENTS

Chapter Two first appeared in a slightly different form in *The Modern Churchman* (now *Modern Believing*) 1987, *29*(1): 15–22, and is reproduced with the kind permission of the Editor.

Chapter Three first appeared in a shorter form in *Contact — Interdisciplinary Journal of Pastoral Studies*, 1976, *3*: 2–8; Chapter Five first appeared in *Contact — Interdisciplinary Journal of Pastoral Studies*, 1991, *2*(105): 2–11; and Chapter Ten first appeared in *Contact — Interdisciplinary Journal of Pastoral Studies*, 1990, *1*(101): 19–27. All three articles are reproduced with the kind permission of the Editor.

Chapter Four was published in 1980 as a monograph by the then British Association for Counselling, and is reproduced with the kind permission of the British Association for Counselling and Psychotherapy.

Chapter Six first appeared for the most part in the then *Journal of Psychodynamic Counselling*, 1996, *2*(1): 55–66; and Chapter Nine in the *Journal of Psychodynamic Practice*, 2007, *13*(4): 385–400, published by Taylor and Francis. These two articles are reproduced with the

CONTENTS

ABOUT THE AUTHOR

Michael Jacobs was for many years Director of the Counselling and Psychotherapy Programme at the University of Leicester, from which post he retired in 2000, moving to Swanage in Dorset. He has been a Visiting Professor at Bournemouth University and is now Visiting Professor in the School of Healthcare, University of Leeds. He has been publishing important texts, often used on training courses, since 1982, the best known being *Psychodynamic Counselling in Action* (third edition, Sage, 2004), and *The Presenting Past* (third edition, Open University Press, 2006). His book on Freud (second edition, Sage, 2003) has been translated into a number of languages. He has also edited some important series, such as "Core concepts in therapy" (Open University Press, 2001–2006), "Counselling skills" (Open University Press, 1995–2005), and the "In search of a therapist" books, featuring over 25 types of therapy (Open University Press, 1995–1996). Important though these books are for those working as counsellors and therapists, he takes particular pride in publications that extend his psychodynamic thinking into other areas, such as his *Illusion, a Psychodynamic Interpretation of Thinking and Belief* (Whurr, 2000), and, with Karnac, *Shakespeare on the Couch* (2008). Michael continues to offer a small therapy and supervision practice, and is in constant demand to lead workshops and address counselling and psychotherapy groups in different parts of the country. But in retirement he also likes to be involved in his local community in ways far removed from his professional life, playing a key role in the local coastwatch, the Swanage Pier, and the Purbeck Film Festival and Arts Week.

PREFACE

Over the course of a career in counselling and psychotherapy I have been privileged to be asked to write, or to have my writing projects welcomed by publishers, with the result that where I am known at all, it is generally for a number of texts that are used in training. This has led to invitations to speak to societies, associations, and groups in the counselling and psychotherapy world—occasions that I have valued in a number of respects. First, they have at times provided me with a topic that the invitation has asked me to speak upon, which has turned my attention to an area about which I may have been thought to know something, but when it came to constructing the lecture soon made me aware that I needed to dig deeper if I was to say anything of value. So, I have been compelled to search the literature, and to examine from my reading of it what my own ideas might be. The process of reading and writing has been an exciting one for me, especially in terms of making sense, to myself and my audience, of what are sometimes complex ideas.

Second, those occasions have given me an audience who, thankfully, answer back, and, if they sometimes ask questions to which I might or might not know the answer, more often than not present opinions that qualify my own and add to my understanding of the subject. This means that, over a number of years, especially if the lecture is delivered again or prepared for publication, I can present a fuller picture than I did to my original audience. These questions that show up gaps in arguments and this interchange of opinion is vital in the quest for further understanding and extension of subjects that can never be exhausted.

However, unlike books, which in many cases become key texts and therefore in first and subsequent editions allow ideas to be disseminated, lectures and papers reach a relatively small audience or readership. Indeed, a major concern I have about the emphasis upon research in universities and psychotherapy/counselling organizations is that, in the case of universities, papers in journals have replaced teaching as the major concern in getting funding, that books, which are of equal value if not more in learning, are no longer the measure of the quality of an academic's work, and that the pursuit of evidence-based research in the therapy world has a tendency to push out the value of the type of factual and speculative scholarship that explores concepts and ideas more than results.

As I come to the close of many years writing (since retirement gives the opportunity to explore new horizons and to become more a learner than a teacher), it is good to be able to collect together in one volume a number of published articles and lectures that I have written over some thirty or more years. They are a selection, since some pieces are too time-bound or too specifically addressed to a particular audience or readership to warrant reproduction in book form. But the papers trace, as my introductions to each I hope show, a restless development as I have come to question aspects of practice and theory.

I have not, of course, ceased that restlessness—indeed, a more private quest allows me to dabble in other disciplines and relate them, where I can, to my fascination with psychoanalytic literature, with less need to present the ideas to a wider world, and therefore in a sense to be more elastic in my thinking. I have always enjoyed thinking, and it is an important part of my therapeutic style as well. There have been times when other therapists seem to me to have wanted to promote feeling rather than thinking, but thinking plays an essential part in processing feelings and in making decisions about when and how to make interventions that will enhance the therapeutic process. I have always felt, even when I have disagreed with some of its arguments, that psychoanalysis provides more material for thinking than any of the other modalities, and this will be obvious from the number of references in this book to Freud and other analysts. My hope is that some of those fascinating ideas that have excited me and that have informed my practice, whether fully understood by me or not, but at any rate processed into my own thinking, will meet and inspire the reader's own desire for unrest.

Michael Jacobs
Swanage
October 2008

CHAPTER ONE

Challenging the stereotype: the psychoanalytic therapist's use of self

T o begin a long way from the beginning . . .

The original papers that constitute this book illustrate aspects of an intellectual journey, but the paper that forms the basis for this chapter, although written far from the start of that journey, may usefully introduce the others. This is partly because it contains sufficient autobiographical references to introduce the writer, whose ideas form the substance of later chapters. It also challenges, as the title suggests, the prejudiced view that many counsellors and therapists, not of a psychodynamic persuasion, have of psychoanalytic and psychodynamic practitioners, perhaps thereby introducing further challenges to theory and practice to which subsequent chapters refer.

*　*　*

Two almost contemporaneous commissions some thirty years into my clinical practice encouraged me to take stock of what sort of person I am and the sort of therapist I am. One was a request to write a chapter in Spinelli and Marshall's book *Embodied Theories* (2001); the other was co-authoring *The Therapist's Use of Self* (2003) with John Rowan. The contributors to *Embodied Theories*, one of whom was also John Rowan, were asked by the editors to "write an account that attempts to examine those features and aspects of their chosen models which significantly inform and clarify their professional lives . . . as well as aspects of their more personal lives" (Spinelli & Marshall, 2001, p. 3). I call myself a psychodynamic therapist, for reasons that I explain below, but I draw upon psychoanalytic theory and practice as my main inspiration; and I found myself reviewing why I had been drawn to that particular model, and how my personality, insofar as I am in any position to assess it, matched my chosen theoretical position. Self-reflection and self-knowledge are an essential part of a therapist's training and ongoing development. But linking this to reflection upon the link between chosen theory and personal life was initially daunting, involving additionally the sort of self-disclosure which is often reckoned to be a thorny area for psychodynamic and psychoanalytic practitioners.

Writing *The Therapist's Use of Self* was equally challenging, partly because of working with an author from a different theoretical position, partly because John Rowan is himself a challenging thinker, but mainly because of the structure of the book, which was suggested by Rowan, drawing its guiding themes from humanistic writers such as Maslow (1987) and Wilber (2000). In that book, one which also linked the person of the therapist with her or his approach, we examined the way therapists use themselves, referring to different modalities (as was the editorial brief), but overarching such references with a template of three ways in which the therapists of any modality might use the self in therapy.

We asked, in a more theoretical way than Spinelli and Marshall had requested their contributors to do, what therapists are like and how they work, as well as who they are behind the role. We acknowledged early on that while there are therapists who are clones of their chosen leader, more Freudian than Freud, more Rogerian than Rogers, nevertheless, within any one orientation, many practitioners have developed their own particular style, their own way of being, a way of expressing themselves that is congruent not only with their approach and with the individual patient or client, but with his or her own self.

We noted the stereotypical picture of different therapies: the Freudian therapist, hidden behind the couch, unseen and often unheard by the patient; the person-centred therapist, consistently positive, speaking in warm tones, deeply empathizing with the client, repeating words and phrases with extra meaning; or the cognitive–behavioural psychologist with a checklist of questions and carefully worked out instructions for exercises to be practised within and outside the session.

In our preliminary discussions, John and I thought that it is not so much that there are alternative ways of being a therapist and of using the self that are capable of being divided into theoretical orientations. Instead, we recognized, as others have also done, that there was much more in common between therapists with a certain degree of experience, whatever their orientation, and that, indeed, the rather different ways in which most therapists use the self are not mutually exclusive. We suggested that there are three main possibilities: the therapist's position can be instrumental, authentic, or transpersonal. Each of these possibilities makes different assumptions about the self, about the therapeutic relationship, and about the level of consciousness involved in doing therapy, and each in turn leads to different assumptions about the content of training and the process of supervision. (Rowan has taken this latter aspect further in a subsequent publication (2005).)

These possibilities or positions might be referred to as levels, although we did not wish to suggest that one way of being was superior to another. There was, none the less and perhaps inevitably, a preference in us for therapists being authentic, since we liked to think of ourselves as being that. There was always going to be some disagreement between us over the transpersonal way of being a therapist, partly because of the use of terms, partly because of the philosophical underpinning of that term, which I was less happy about than Rowan. But a measure of the understanding that grew between us in the writing of the book is contained in two brief comments in our final chapter, where, in dialogue, Rowan writes:

What was . . . curious, at least to me, is that the psychodynamic theorists, who are often thought by others to be rather rigid and hidebound, came through . . . as having a great deal to say about the authentic and spontaneous, while I replied,

> As you have learned from the psychoanalytic/psychodynamic, I
> have also learned from the humanistic, and particularly the
> transpersonal. [Rowan & Jacobs, 2003, p. 116]

I concentrate here on the authentic therapist because authenticity is not a term that appears with much frequency in psychoanalytic writing. A search of the word as a descriptor of a therapist or analyst in a large number of psychoanalytic journals throws up very few instances of its use, and the only person who most obviously employs the term is Peter Lomas—once a psychoanalyst, but one who parted company with the British Psychoanalytic Society over the rigidity of training and the emphasis on analytic technique.

To highlight the marks of the authentic therapist, some description must be given of the other two ways of being, the instrumental and the transpersonal. Where the therapist is in the instrumental position, the client is usually regarded as someone who has problems, which problems need to be put right (either by the client, or by the therapist, or by both). This can lead to the therapist acting in a somewhat programmed way. Technical ability is regarded as something both possible and desirable. But, while this may appear to verge upon a caricature of cognitive–behavioural therapy, rational emotive behaviour therapy, or neuro-linguistic programming, and especially likely to be attractive in time-limited work, that is far too narrow an interpretation of the instrumental. It is equally possible for an instrumental use of self to be present in long- or short-term therapy, in a self-disclosing or blank screen approach, and whether or not transference or the unconscious are felt to be important concepts. This is because the instrumental can be defined as learning about a technique and applying a technique, and the technique being the most important aspect of the work. In a sense, what the instrumental therapist does is to put technique before self, whether it be the cognitive–behavioural therapist who has researched the value of specific interventions, or the analytic therapist who tries to prevent countertransference feelings from interfering with the neutrality of the analytic stance, or the person-centred therapist who is concerned above all to demonstrate the core conditions, and concentrate entirely upon what the client is experiencing. The therapist, of whatever modality, concentrates on delivering the technique that he or she has learnt, and has not adapted to a more personalized way of working.

Indeed, it appears that this might be an obvious way of describing the psychoanalyst's use of self, which can be illustrated in a number of ways. First, there is a set of techniques—originally laid out by Freud between 1911 and 1915 in his various "Papers on Technique", but developed further over time to include the importance of a neutral blank screen, minimal responses, designed to encourage the patient to free associate, the promotion of conditions to highlight the transference, and the systematic analysis of resistance. Some theorists (e.g., Kernberg, 1975; Rangell, 1954) treat the unconscious of the therapist as a tool, something to be ordered and disciplined. The main purpose of the training analysis is to reduce the self of the therapist, both in the conscious and the unconscious, to something usable technically. Countertransference is principally understood as that which blocks the therapist from being able to identify what the patient is feeling, or which leads to projection on to the patient of the therapist's own feelings. So Rangell, in describing psychoanalysis, writes,

> Psychoanalysis is a method of therapy whereby conditions are brought about favorable for the development of a transference neurosis, in which the past is restored in the present, in order that, through a systematic interpretative attack on the resistances which oppose it, there occurs a resolution of that neurosis (transference and infantile) to the end of bringing about structural changes in the mental apparatus of the patient to make the latter capable of optimum adaptation to life. [1954, pp. 739–40]

In effect the analyst is left as a thinker—a true *analyst*—untroubled by emotions or unconscious thoughts that would otherwise interfere with the "pure gold of analysis" (Freud, 1919a, p. 168). Freud promoted the neutrality of the analyst for a number of good reasons, one of them perhaps being fear of the potential damage that can be caused by countertransference. But the abstinence of the analyst was also felt to motivate the patient, although in the following passage we see the interests of the analyst as well:

> I cannot advise my colleagues too urgently to model themselves during psychoanalytic treatment on the surgeon who puts aside all his feelings, even his human sympathy . . . The justification for

> requiring this emotional coldness in the analyst is that it creates the most advantageous conditions for both parties: for the doctor a desirable protection for his own emotional life and for the patient the largest amount of help that we can give him today. [Freud, 1912e, p. 115]

Such a passage provides one of the reasons why I prefer to use "psychodynamic" as a professional label rather than "psychoanalytic": "dynamic" expresses so much more richly what passes between therapist and patient, as well as, of course, within the psyche, whereas "analytic" suggests the medical dissection of the psyche on the operating table, or detailed scrutiny of the psyche under the microscope.

However, it is not my intention to deny that becoming a good therapeutic instrument is part of the training and practice of a therapist. The need to be objective in this instrumental way is as important as it is in the authentic position to welcome subjective experience into the consulting room. To be an instrument has some similarity to the phrase attributed to Francis of Assisi, "Make me an instrument of thy peace"; the therapist becomes a means through which healing might be transmitted. But there are, none the less, many good reasons why the therapist's use of self should not stop there.

In writing the chapter for *Embodied Theories*, I needed, of course, to reflect on how my theoretical stance and my personality related. As I looked back, I saw how much this instrumental way of working had appealed to me at the beginning of my training and career. I am not sure even now whether I chose to study psychoanalysis or whether psychoanalysis chose me. It represented a substantial body of knowledge, one that provided an alternative to my first discipline, which had been theology, a discourse that had once sustained my intellectual interest and my emotional fervour but that had, over a number of years and with exposure to other paradigms, begun to lose its viability and its veracity for me. Psychoanalysis asked similar questions, if phrased rather differently, to those addressed by religion. Freud, too, had wanted "to understand something of the riddles of the world in which we live" (1927a, p. 247), just as I had been previously engaged in a religious quest to solve the riddles of existence and the universe.

What I did not see at the time that I forsook theology for psycho-analysis, but became so much more obvious to me later, was that psychoanalysis also appealed because it was cultic like the church (although this cultic status is true of other therapies). Therapists and counsellors often feel passionate about their therapeutic schools and positions, and I was no exception. Psychoanalysis beckoned with a type of certainty. It had its dogmas; indeed, as I began to discover, it had its creeds (Freud, 1923a, p. 247), and in some psychoanalytic circles woe betide the person who tried to step outside them. It had a whole set of moral views—although they are called "psychopathology" rather than "sin". I could "analyse" people rather than hear their confessions. I could help relieve their guilt, rather than pronounce forgiveness. I could achieve a new kind of status, because as the status of clergy declined the admiration of counsellors and therapists appeared to grow.

I exaggerate slightly, but only in order to make the point. Psychoanalysis suited me: it fitted, if not quite like a glove, at least enough to support my personal characteristics. Indeed, what is ironical is that I left the church because I experienced it as dogmatic, intolerant, and narrow in much of its public thinking, and I felt that it had no place for my more radical questioning and independent mind, for my "desire of unrest". That I should then have allied myself to psychoanalysis is now not at all surprising, given the power of "the return of the repressed", one of Freud's most insightful phrases (e.g., 1913i, p. 323—Freud denies there that the return of the repressed is seen in character formation, but I cannot agree with him). In some ways I went from the frying pan to the fire.

But not completely, because for my part the "return of the repressed", perhaps more accurately "the return of the suppressed", also applied to my free-thinking spirit. If I was on the one hand rather conformist—public school, Oxford, and the church—on the other I had always been uncomfortable with the conformity of others and of institutions: a careful rebel at school, somewhat radical in the church, and later becoming an independent voice within psychodynamic psychotherapy. But how easy it might have been, perhaps even was, for psychoanalysis to entrap me, to turn me into a stereotypical analytic therapist. I was fortunate, because I never undertook a prescribed "training" as such, and fortunate too that I worked 100 miles from London. Fortunate, because training with a psychoanalytic society or association, or so it has often seemed to me, especially in London, tends to produce a way of thinking that finds it difficult to question accepted wisdom, both of theory and practice, or makes it very difficult to voice this within what remains a largely conservative profession. That is the other reason why I prefer to avoid the title psychoanalytic, since it has connotations of rigidity, of intolerance, and of superiority over other therapeutic approaches. There are of course exceptions to this generalization, some of which I refer to below, but institutions have a tendency to progress at the speed of the slowest.

Nevertheless, when I was writing my chapter in *Embodied Theories*, and later still when I was working with Rowan on the theme of the authentic use of self from a psychoanalytic perspective, I began to wonder whether my view of the dogmatism and certainties of psychoanalysis had also been partly my own projection. Or was it, indeed, something that I had genuinely experienced in analysts or introjected from analysts whom I had known, heard, or read? I suspect the answer lies somewhere in the interplay of these different forces, and the precise proportion of projection and introjection does not matter to me. Projections have an element of the reality of the other, even if they emanate primarily from the self.

There were other ways in which psychoanalysis initially met my needs. Like the priest in the pulpit, the therapist is placed at a safe distance from parishioner or patient. This place is partly professional, and I have no wish to see it or practise it in any other way than by being completely professional. I still value this distancing and discreteness in psychodynamic therapy. But, at the same time, the chosen stance in my early days protected me from becoming too involved; not so much in the transference and countertransference, which remain very useful concepts even if sometimes they are ways of denying the reality of the therapist–client relationship, but in terms of sharing what Lomas calls "the ordinary human response" (1973, p. 15). This was strange, because this distant stance was not the example set by my own therapist, himself a leading analyst. It was a projection of mine on to the admonitions about practice, which was not without foundation (because the literature is full of it), but one which then suited me. I made this projection without testing (or indeed seeing with my own eyes) whether this was really the way psychoanalytic therapists behave. My projection supported my personal need. And, for a while in those early days, I became much more withdrawn socially, as if the observing, careful, non-disclosing therapist had leaked into my life outside the consulting room. I think now this was because I needed to find a new identity as a therapist in place of being a priest, and therefore needed to hide in my shell until that identity was firm enough to risk its fuller exposure.

I suspect that my motives for wanting to be a psychoanalytic therapist, as in those days I wished I could call myself, are not peculiar. But, at the same time, I want here to challenge the stereotypical view of the psychoanalyst as being totally instrumental and without authenticity. Not only was my own therapist quite unlike the stereotype; there are a large number of stories and episodes about many of the leading names in psychoanalysis, either in their own writing, or recorded by those who have been in therapy with them, which support that challenge. I share a few of them with you.

While a young student at Vienna University, Bruno Goetz experienced occasional attacks of acute migraines, and was referred to Freud, who at that time was relatively unknown. The first two meetings so shook him that when he returned home he wrote them down, sending a verbatim of the sessions to a friend. At the end of the first session, Freud had given the young man 200 crowns, because Goetz's father could not afford to pay for his son's studies. The migraines cleared up after the first interview, and Goetz responded to an invitation to return in order to thank Freud. Goetz describes the end of the second interview, and how Freud said to him,

> The older I grow the more mistrustful I become. I don't want to impose my ideas on you: you are very young and the devil knows where you will end up . . . You must try out your own way . . . What I have been saying to you just now is not scientific and it has done me good to play with ideas a bit, instead of continually imposing a strict discipline on myself. The serious business of your life will be in a totally different sphere, and your good conscience will be of a different kind. The main thing is never to lose heart. And *never* have yourself analysed. Write good poetry, if it is in your power to do so, but don't become shut in on yourself or hide yourself away. One always stands naked before God: that is the only prayer we can still offer.

Goetz goes on,

> I returned home confused and shaken and was unable to sleep that night. That is why I have written you this letter, so that you can form a picture of this great healer of souls and so that you can imagine my present dilemma.

> . . . A few months later I moved to Munich to continue my studies at the university there. I went to say goodbye to Freud. It was the last time I saw him. I didn't send my friend an account of the visit, or, if I did, I didn't keep an abstract of my letter, so that I can longer quote verbatim.

> All I still remember is that Freud, who had read a few minor articles of mine which had appeared in a newspaper, found a great deal to criticize in them. He warned me against confusing intellectual argument with poetry, saying that in these articles my head had slipped into my heart and my heart had slipped into my head, and also that I had obviously been influenced by his modes of thought—which didn't suit me. He thought that it would be a good thing if we were not to meet for a while, nor should I write to him, since he would only confuse me. A real encounter such as ours was one which transcended any separation. But I was no theoretician, and so he advised me to engage in theoretical discussions only when absolutely obliged to do so; I should stick to my last and write stories and poetry: that would unite us much more closely than any encounter in the realm of abstract discussion.

> I have no idea what I said in reply. When he shook hands with me as I was leaving, he looked straight at me, and once again I felt the tender, sad warmth of his gaze. The memory of that look has remained with me all my life. [Goetz, 1975, pp. 138–43]

We might want to argue that this was not actually analysis, although there is similar evidence of the authentic Freud in, for example, his own account of the Rat Man, where, as in other recorded case histories, he appears not to have kept slavishly to what we have taken to be his own technical rules. He was far less opaque than, in "The Papers on Technique", he would have others be. In the account of the Rat Man, just as one example, Freud describes how

> I told him . . . his youth was very much in his favour, as well as the intactness of his personality. In this connection I said a word or two

upon the good opinion I had formed of him, and this gave him visible pleasure. [1909d, p. 178—in Freud's original notes of this session Freud actually says that he complimented the young man, see Lipton, 1979]

Is this just reassurance, delivered as a technical piece of ego-support? I doubt it. Similar examples of Freud's obvious personal involvement in the therapeutic conversation were remembered by the patient known as the Wolf Man, when he was interviewed by Obholzer. He remembered how Freud explained to him the reason for his seating position, that a girl had once tried to seduce him when he sat elsewhere. Freud sometimes gave his views: "He discussed painting and that a son of his had wanted to become a painter, that he gave up that idea and become an architect" (Obholzer, 1980, pp. 33–34). Freud helped him out occasionally with money (*ibid.*, pp. 60–61). Lampl-de Groot describes how it was when working with Freud that she realized that in addition to the transference relationship, there was a "real" relationship between the patient and the analyst. She writes, "I feel that Freud's carefully selected alternation of 'strict neutrality' and human relatedness has definitely influenced my personal attitude and behavior as an analyst" (1976, p. 284).

Such personal accounts suggest that the analysts whom we might either idealize or demonize (as many counsellors and therapists either within or outside the psychodynamic modality do) are much more ordinary than our transferences allow them to be. Arthur Couch, when in a training analysis with Anna Freud, writes of several ordinary human moments, including Anna Freud's knitting throughout the sessions. Here is one such episode:

Another memorable episode happened at the end of several sessions where I had been telling of my frustrations with my first training case at the Institute. The patient was a young woman who was not only very depressed, but also very soft-spoken—so soft that I could barely hear her words and missed some of them, to my concern. With the help of my supervisor, I had tried out a number of interpretations in an attempt to solve this symptomatic soft whispering with me. Some attempts were made to interpret it as resistance: for example, the patient was afraid of my reproach about her thoughts; or she felt guilty about them herself; or that all material was like sexual secrets; or that she didn't want me to hear anything about her, and so forth. I even tried some early (for me) transference interpretations along the lines that she wanted me to move physically closer to her to share her intimate feelings: or to comfort her; or to reassure her that I was concerned; and so forth. As I recounted these various failed attempts each day, Anna Freud seemed to increase the intensity of her knitting, which she did most of the time so silently that I hardly noticed it. Finally in one session, she began to speak about the issue of my soft-spoken patient. I expected her to give a very important interpretation about my diffi-cult situation. But what Anna Freud said was simply: "Tell her to speak up". This I did, and it solved that particular problem for the rest of a long analysis. [Couch, 1995, p. 160]

There are many other such examples, only a few of which need be referred to here: Harold Searles (1965) demonstrates in his papers the openness of his personal responses to his patients, and his honesty about his own feelings, some of which were clearly shared when it felt appropriate. There are frequent references to be found in Winnicott's work, whether as recorded by him, or in the lengthier accounts by Margaret Little (1990), or here from Harry Guntrip's description:

[Winnicott's] consulting room was simple, restful in colours, unos-tentatious, carefully planned, so Mrs Winnicott told me, to put the patient at ease. I would knock and walk in, and presently Winnicott would stroll in with a cup of tea in his hand and a cheery "Hallo", and sit on a small wooden chair by the couch. I would sit down on the couch sideways or lie down as I felt inclined, and change posi-tion freely according to how I felt or what I was saying. Always at the end, as I departed, he held out his hand for a friendly hand-shake. [1996, p. 745]

Or we might draw in turn upon the reminiscences of one who was in analysis with Guntrip:

In a crisis time he sent a postcard from holidays. At a public meet-ing he was careful to notice me and have a natural meeting. Touch was limited but kept for meaning—at a crisis—a held hand and a look in the eye spoke empathy. [Kidd, undated]

Even the Kleinians cannot be pigeon-holed, as Hill's account shows, the title of which itself challenges the stereotype: "Am I a

Kleinian? Is anyone?" (1993). He describes his experience of being in therapy with three Kleinian analysts, each of whom had a quite different style and manner. Masud Khan's case studies (e.g., 1974, 1983), which have an element of showmanship about them, demonstrate what is at times a startlingly unorthodox approach to his patients. It has to be recognized that in the end he overstepped the mark, and authenticity became abuse, and it is perhaps fear of this that keeps some practitioners too purist. Rather differently in the fictionalized *A Guard Within* (Ferguson, 1973), the Jungian Robert Moody shows the same type of care of Sarah Ferguson that Winnicott did of Margaret Little. It is a case that ended tragically, perhaps because of Moody's premature death, and so shows the danger of over-involvement, but it none the less supports the challenge to the stereotypical view.

Then there is the ongoing critique of psychoanalytic technique that runs through all Peter Lomas's writing (e.g., 1973). Lomas felt compelled to sever his connections with the British Psychoanalytic Society, although he still identifies his approach as basically psychoanalytic, with a small "p". I hesitate to include Yalom (1991; and Yalom & Elkin, 1974), who is more properly styled an existential therapist, although his theoretical position includes much that would be familiar to a psychodynamic therapist. His case studies show an obvious authenticity.

As Rowan and I came to the end of our writing, and engaged in the dialogue that concludes our book, I found myself wanting to address a particular question about authenticity. I was thinking of Guntrip's analysis, not in this instance with Winnicott, where there is no doubt that Winnicott is far from stereotypical, but his first analysis with Fairbairn (Guntrip, 1996). The word "authentic" appears to mean a style of being as a therapist which involves openness to the "real" self, which in turn probably means some self-disclosure, and may even include at times being more active. But "authentic" can also mean "true to oneself" and if we recognize, as we surely must, that psychoanalysts are trying to be as true to themselves as much any other therapists, is there any reason why the relatively silent analyst should be any the less authentic? Authenticity comes from the way a person *is* as much as the way they act or speak. So is not the more passive analyst also authentic, true to himself or herself, not only because he or she believes a particular style, and stays true to that belief, but also because it suits that person's own way of being? He or she is not adopting a role.

The interaction between Guntrip and Fairbairn merits closer attention. Fairbairn once said to Guntrip:

> You can go on analysing for ever and get no-where. It's the personal relation that is therapeutic. Science has no values except scientific values, the schizoid values of the investigator who stands outside of life and watches. It is purely instrumental, useful for a time but then you have to get back to living. [Guntrip, 1996, p. 741]

Note the word "instrumental", which Fairbairn contrasts with the personal relationship of therapy.

Yet, as Guntrip describes, although this was Fairbairn's stated view

> of the "mirror analyst", a non-relating observer simply interpreting . . . in spite of his conviction Fairbairn did not have the same capacity for natural, spontaneous "personal relating" that Winnicott had. With me he was more of a "technical interpreter" than he thought he was, or than I expected. [*ibid.*, pp. 741–742]

Guntrip writes of Fairbairn's consulting room and the seating arrangements, Fairbairn sitting

> behind a large flat-topped desk, I used to think "in state" . . . I used to think he could reach over the desk and hit me on the head . . . odd for an analyst who did not believe in the "mirror-analyst" theory. [*ibid.*, p. 744)]

It is interesting that Guntrip chose the couch, not realizing that he could as well have sat on the small settee at the side of the desk, which eventually he did—perhaps his own stereotype influenced that choice. It is also significant that if Fairbairn was formal in sessions, the two men met after the sessions and "discussed theory and he would unbend"—itself quite a break with traditional boundaries. Guntrip tells how he saw "the human Fairbairn as we talked face to face". And when they parted for the last time, Guntrip writes

> I suddenly realised that in all that long period we had never once shaken hands, and he was letting me leave without that friendly

gesture. I put out my hand and at once he took it, and I suddenly saw a few tears trickle down his face. *I saw the warm heart of this man with a fine mind and a shy nature.* [*ibid.*, p. 745, Guntrip's italics]

So was Fairbairn suppressing his warm heart when he was in the role of the analyst? Or is he, as I tried to argue with John Rowan, also showing a type of authenticity that Guntrip, partly in his own enthusiasm perhaps to have a "proper analysis", did not initially see. Guntrip certainly acknowledges his own part in creating the formality. I have no reason to doubt Fairbairn's genuineness. My sense is that Fairbairn did not adopt that style as an analyst, but that he was being truly Fairbairn. I have no way of being able to prove it, but reading Guntrip's article, I have no doubt that Fairbairn's soul was there, and that his silent, interpretive stance was not the mark of the purely instrumental, but an indication of the authentic "shy nature" of the man.

Guntrip's account raises a number of questions about authenticity and instrumentality. He is certainly critical of his analysis with Fairbairn: he could not, for example, accept the constant stream of oedipal interpretations, although through Guntrip's negative response he really understood how dominating his own mother was, and he appears to have gained much from the analysis. When he went on to see Winnicott, he gained a different perspective, enabling Guntrip to find "an ultimate good mother" (*ibid.*, p. 749). But Guntrip's more complete healing came after both men were dead. So if we ask, as many have done and still do, what makes for effective therapy (and that is the point of Guntrip's article), we might say that both analysts helped, the instrumental and the authentic, but in the end it was a powerful dream, the night after Guntrip had learnt of Winnicott's death, that enabled the ultimate shift to take place.

My co-author disagreed with me as I rehearsed these arguments in discussion, suggesting that I was fighting against any real separation between the instrumental and the authentic forms of consciousness. Rowan argues that there is a great gap between the instrumental and the authentic, such that most people live and work at the instrumental level, and have little or no authentic awareness, and that this is true of therapists as well.

I recognize that there is indeed a gap between the instrumental and the authentic, although Rowan and I also felt that each had their place in the work of every therapist. I can see the way a therapist can move between the two ways of being, and can also be caught up (since it is less an act of will) in the transpersonal.

The transpersonal use of self is the third way of being as a therapist. Here again there is increasing evidence that, while not being conventionally spiritual, or at least spiritual in the sense that many transpersonal therapists are, there are psychoanalytic and psychodynamic therapists who really engage at this level. But it is a way of being that partly has to develop, and partly breaks in from outside, if we can permit it. When I first began to practise, "not knowing" made me extremely anxious. The accepted therapist stance of saying little and turning questions back to the client enabled me to mask any lack of knowledge, and perhaps to hide much of my anxiety. It was much later that I could be content in uncertainty, or even find excitement in the assurance that where there is uncertainty there is always the possibility of finding something new. With this came the discovery of Bion's phrase "without memory or desire" (1967), a phrase I came across long after I had originally trained, although I doubt if it would have made any real sense to me had I heard of it earlier. Similarly, I re-discovered "unknowing" (or, more accurately, to adapt Eliot's phrase, arrived where I started and "knew" for the first time). I had been familiar with "unknowing" from a special study of mystic literature when reading theology (see also Jacobs, 2000a). So I began to appreciate the significance of Winnicott's profound ability to tolerate gaps in his knowledge, and his emphasis on the creativity of "the space between". His notion of inner space, and the "for ever silent" central self out of which "communication naturally arises" (1965, p. 192) have become an essential "credo" for me, without having to make it, as once I might, into a creed. But I had to be ready first for Winnicott and for Bion. I had to reach a point where their words described what I was already experiencing in my work before I could appreciate their true value.

The chapters that follow show some of this intellectual journey. I have been through a series of illusions such as I describe elsewhere (Jacobs, 2000a). With regard to psychoanalysis, at first I embraced, perhaps even clung to, its supposed methods and theory, before discovering as I questioned that many others had also questioned and aided the development of this richest of veins of thought in the therapy world. I realized that what I initially learned was one-sided, and that there are other ways of being a therapist, which the examples above clearly demonstrate. Perhaps we discover Searles, Winnicott, Lomas, and even the real person behind Freud, only when we are ready for them. Searles, for example, recounts how when he first experienced his oedipal countertransference, his training told him that he was not yet sufficiently analysed (1965, p. 285). But, as he explored his fantasies of love for his patients, he found in private conversations with other analysts that what they actually experienced with patients was somewhat different from what they were prepared to say in public. I early on read Lomas's *True and False Experience* (1973), and indeed had a long meeting with him, although it was some fifteen years later that I really took notice of his own search for authenticity, and particularly his own embodiment of being "ordinary". Sometimes questioning leads to unlearning, but also to discovering that we had not yet learnt enough of what was already obviously there, but which we were not yet ready to recognize.

There is a further aspect that needs to be taken into account: that authenticity is not just the way the therapist is and acts, but is also the product of a therapeutic relationship. There are some clients where it is possible to be more authentic, to be more oneself, where the therapist's responses and interventions reflect the way the therapist is experiencing them; and there are other clients who make it impossible to be authentic, where a therapist has to be on guard as to what he or she can say. Perhaps that is the wrong way of putting it: rather that with some clients it is authentic for a therapist to be one way, and with other clients it is authentic to be another way. That, in turn, might depend upon whether the clients are themselves reaching a point of greater authenticity. Those who present a "false self", and who are frightened of what may happen when the false self is taken away, are the clients who need their therapist to be much more circumspect in the way the therapist is with them, and in what can be said to them, and who might even, commenting upon us as therapists, tell others that we are distant, say little, and are not much help. Conversely, those who have allowed themselves to give up much of the pretence they have had about themselves and others are the clients where it feels possible to be more "oneself".

Whatever reservations I have about psychoanalytic politics and institutions, psychoanalysis has provided me with the resources to uncover the position to which I have been moving. Dipping into the vast treasury of writing from a psychoanalytic perspective has enabled me to find that there are indeed many other analysts and therapists who appear to think along similar lines. Psychoanalysis has its pockets of conservatism, indeed, and it has its fair share of rather cloned practitioners who are afraid to question what they have been taught, or what their personal therapist has modelled for them by way of practice. It also has others (and I have come across many of these) who wait for permission to express their doubts and uncertainties, not having learnt that it is safe to do so in their training.

I do not, therefore, dismiss the stereotype of the psychoanalytic therapist, but I have enough evidence from my own development as a therapist and in the practice of others more experienced than myself to want to challenge it. I have not raised here why we should cling to stereotypes, whether they are used in criticism of other therapeutic orientations or as patterns for entrenchment within orientations. But I do suggest that we may see what we want to see.

What I do challenge is the standard caricature of psychoanalytic practice. I do this not just to suggest those whose practice is based upon other modalities that they may care to look rather more deeply at what they think they see. I write just as much for those within psychoanalytic and psychodynamic therapy, whether trainers, therapists, supervisors, or students, to those who believe and perpetuate the stereotype: some of your luminaries and many of your colleagues are not so ready to conform.

CHAPTER TWO

Our desire of unrest

T
he influence and the ongoing relevance of some of my theological education become obvious in a number of the papers
I have written. For those not familiar with the use of biblical
sources, I do not regard the "truth", whether historical or doctrinal,
as important but, rather, the significance of the metaphor or the
symbolic use of the language. This is especially true in reading the
paper that forms the basis of this chapter, delivered first to a theological society at Manchester University, and published subsequently in the journal then titled *The Modern Churchman* (Jacobs,
1987). It is the theme that is important, whether addressed to
theologians, therapists, or others. That the theme resonates for me
many years on from its inception is instanced not only in taking the
paper's title as the title of this book, but that it is explicitly or
implicitly present in most of my papers.

*   *   *

Although there are some who live in apparent chaos, or whose lives
appear chaotic, most people do not like too much disorder. Some
(particularly those who are possessed of an obsessional personality)

do not like it at all. This is not surprising, since from early infancy we seek a sense of security in a bewildering world and erect safe defences against what can be at times terrifying experiences that threaten to disrupt our equilibrium.

Parents usually try to provide security, including, among many other things, reading stories to their younger children at bedtime, partly in order to settle the insecurities of the day and partly to prepare them to overcome the terrors of the night. In sleep the dream functions as another type of story, the function of which, as Freud saw (1925i, p. 127), includes preserving sleep and enabling us to rest; at the same time the dream seeks to order or re-order those feelings that still trouble us from the day just passed.

Myth also orders the confusion of humanity's experience of the natural world and its anxieties about the supernatural. Throughout time it has been, and remains, one of the functions of the intellectual (whether scientist or theologian) to attempt to order chaos, which task, on a more academic level, is echoed in the way the therapist and counsellor undertake a similar task in the private sphere with the troubled client. Freud (1907b) and Fromm (1967) each see a parallel between the universal and the private when they link religion and obsessional neurosis, an attempt in both its private and public form to exert some control in the face of disordered and troubled thinking and behaviour. The danger in all these activities, whether scientific, therapeutic, or spiritual, it is argued here, lies not so much in chaos itself, but to imagine that chaos can ever be tamed. When we do that or think we have done that, we lose the creativity that comes from the tension between order and chaos.

A case example illustrates the individual level.

Paul was studying to be a doctor, but had failed his exams in the final year. When he came to see the university counsellor he doubted whether he wanted to be a doctor at all. He explained that he found himself becoming anxious in the face of incurable illness. Over the course of a number of sessions it became clear that he found it difficult to tolerate situations that he could not control. A past girlfriend had told him that his trouble was that he thought he was God. Indeed, one of the reasons for that relationship ending was because he wanted everything his own way.

Paul wondered whether there was any truth in what his former girl-friend had said; she had also said that he had cared about patients in general but did not care for them as individuals. This last remark hurt, because he cared so much about patients who were incurable that he tended to become anxious and depressed. Nevertheless, there was some truth in what she had said. Paul's care was evident as long as he felt himself to be a member of a profession that had the general aim of curing illness, but he found it difficult to be a caring doctor to the patient who could not be cured. At such times he was reminded that he was not God, and in one session he recalled the time when he was helpless himself, when he had been ill as a child, and how this also paralleled the helplessness he felt about his parents, who were unhappy people who felt life always had shades of doom hanging over it. Paul's real problem was not the mask of god-like status that the medical profession offered to confer upon him, but in being able to tolerate the uncontrollable in life, and the uncontrollable in his patients.

The god-like status of doctors is, of course, one of the jibes that those who envy their position and power can throw at them, but there are plenty of other professionals who can feel the same way about themselves. At such times it does every professional good to be reminded of God's reply to Job in the nature-hymn at the end of their dialogue, where the creator's first speech (Job 38–39) as good as asks Job just who he thinks he is. "Can you order creation? Do you understand its ways? Who is God? You or me?"—such is the clear rebuke. Setting ourselves up as gods is a professional hazard, with plenty of warnings against such presumption in both the Old and the New Testaments.

Nevertheless, we might argue with Job's God that elsewhere humanity is told that it shares in the task of creation, or at least in its ordering (Genesis 2). Tolkien has used the phrase "sub-creator". And, while alluding to the Old Testament creation myth, the ancient legends upon which it draws speak less of creation out of the void as of creation out of chaos; indeed, of a massive fight between two forces, which we might think of as order and chaos. In the task of sub-creation a clear place needs to be made for the recognition of chaos, not simply of order. Thinkers generally, whether theologians or therapists or theorists generally, can only engage in the task creating order if they are prepared to enter the chaos out of which order is created.

This injunction is addressed to me as much as to anyone else. Like other writers, I often reflect upon the creative process itself. I start with an idea, although it may not be anything as grand as the notion of an idea suggests. Perhaps it is better described as an uncomfortable feeling, a sort of intellectual itch: in this case it is that the concept of order needs attention and indeed some questioning. I do not know where this idea or itch will take me, but out of random and often chaotic thoughts, through chasing ideas (often unsuccessfully) in other literature, and despite moments of greatest doubt that anything will emerge, or whether indeed it is worth going on, there comes a vague sense of direction, a pathway through the chaos, which I have to order sufficiently to communicate to another person. But the ideas that form must not become so ordered that I fall into the very trap that I am trying to avoid, that of making chaos too safe. If there is to be continuous creation, we must permit continuing chaos.

Yet, if this is true of the creative process, it does not seem to follow that the finished work, in its resolution, allows for chaos. There might, however, be plenty of chaos before the resolution; for example, in some of the stories that children are told. These stories, like some myths, take as their material the chaotic internal world of phantasy and attempt to resolve the inner conflict through fantasy (note the difference in spelling in here, which follows classical psychoanalytic terminology: phantasy representing ideas in the unconscious, fantasy a literary form). Fairy stories, as Bettelheim (1978) interprets them, are constructed around primitive fears and phantasies—being eaten by witches, facing terrifying monsters, overcoming evil, working towards an ending that normally brings consolation and resolution. Stories loved by older children, as the Rustins (1987) amply illustrate, are "ways of representing some themes of emotional experience and crises in childhood in imaginative and poetic terms" (*ibid.*, p. 2).

It is not only traditional fairy stories that draw upon primitive fears and phantasies. An example, which incidentally illustrates Kleinian theories as I have observed elsewhere (Jacobs, 2006, pp. 83–84), is Maurice Sendak's *Where the Wild Things Are*, in which a wild-tempered young boy, Max, sent to bed without his supper because of his behaviour, in a dream faces his inner wildness, symbolized as a group of terrible and terrifying monsters. Max tames them, becomes king of the wild things, and eventually returns from his dream adventure, having resolved his wildness, and finding the consolation of his supper waiting for him, still hot (Sendak, 1970).

This is, of course, in common with nearly all fairy stories, a story that concludes with a satisfying resolution. Tolkien, in his essay on fairy stories, says that all complete fairy stories must have "the Consolation of the Happy Ending" (1964, p. 66). He coins a word to describe this: "eucatastrophe"—an overturning of all that has gone before, an overturning for good. Eucatastrophe is the opposite of catastrophe, in which good things are overturned by disaster. A "piercing glimpse of joy" (*ibid.*, p. 61) comes at the climax of the story, as in one of the stories of the master of faerie, Andrew Lang, "Each knight came alive and lifted his sword, and shouted 'Long live (the) Prince'" (*ibid.*, pp. 60–61). In comparison with that, writes Tolkien, the words "happily ever after" are just the margin of the picture.

What Tolkien observes as integral to the literary form of the fairy story is also true of many of the other stories we read, or watch in dramatic form. Many novels feature conflict and struggle, love lost and love won. They, too, have their happy endings: lovers marry, the spy is exposed, the detective solves the case, or the forces of good in a distant universe win over evil. Tragedy is, of course, not at all like that, and indeed Tolkien places it as a form diametrically opposite the fairy story. But even in tragedy there is more often than not a resolution, albeit a bloody one. The wrong decisions made early in the story lead in an almost ordered and predictable way to the tragic conclusion. Tragedy has its own logic, often an order above humankind that is at first defied, but in the end reasserts itself at the cost of the hero, anti-hero, or heroine. Even in much Elizabethan and Jacobean tragedy, when we may be left with bodies lying all over the stage, death is a neat ending, enabling us to bury the experience. There is no tension in entropy.

I do not know if others feel similarly, but I find the most disturbing literature, whether it is in the novel or in dramatic form, is that which is perhaps a phenomenon of our own times, where the end is not an ending at all, but is a beginning that leaves us in doubt about what happens next. We are left with our fantasies; we are left puzzled, confused, and uncomfortable. For example, Iris Murdoch concludes her novel *The Sea, The Sea* with a casket—alluded to throughout the book and which may or may not contain a demon—

falling to the floor. There follow the words: "The lid has come off and whatever was inside it has certainly got out. Upon the demon-ridden pilgrimage of human life, what next I wonder?" (1978).

Some stories therefore do not end "happily ever after". And although Tolkien observes that the Gospel contains a fairy story, "a story of a much larger kind that embraces all the essence of fairy stories" (1964, p. 62), the resurrection of Christ is what Tolkien terms the eucatastrophe (*ibid.*, p. 60). It is the happy ending. Yet the apparently original ending of Mark's Gospel, or perhaps the most original we know of, contains the enigmatic description of the disciples at the empty tomb: "for they were afraid" (Mark 16: 8). There are two versions of the creation myth in the opening chapters of Genesis. That ascribed to the priestly author conveys the message of order out of chaos, but misses out the more untidy ending of the Jahwist author's account. The book of Job is certainly about tragedy, but the epilogue, with its idyllic ending, leaves many readers cold and discontented with a false resolution, as if the later additions to the book cannot leave Job in chaos. New Testament scholars (e.g., Jeremias, 1966) have also suggested that the authors of the first three gospels cannot leave the parables to stand as they might well have been told, with the listeners having to work out their own meaning. The gospel writers have added allegorical interpretations, having to drive home their own interpretations.

The passion for order, which Fromm implies takes the form of an obsession with dogma in post-Constantinian Christianity (1964, p. 68), seems to be instanced in the intense theological debates about the nature of Christ, the Trinity, right through to transubstantiation, infallibility, and the like. When an iota can divide Christendom, and shibboleths can send men to their death, the need for order has prevailed over doubt and chaos in the most disastrous way. While I do not doubt that many of the great theologians have struggled with ideas, the church, like other institutions, elevates its thinkers into dogmatists, so that what, in Freud's judgement,

> are given out as teachings . . . [a]nswers to the riddles that tempt the curiosity of man, such as how the universe began or what is the relation between body and mind, are developed in conformity with the underlying assumptions of this system. It is an enormous relief to the individual psyche if the conflicts of its childhood . . . conflicts

which it has never wholly overcome—are removed from it and brought to a solution which is universally accepted. [Freud, 1927c, p. 30]

Yet Freud recognized that religious thinkers must have had their doubts, even if they were forced to suppress them (*ibid.*, p. 27). Perhaps rather than doubt, faith in the value of chaos is an alternative, as Sarah Maitland, a feminist novelist whose work is shot through with theological concepts, affirms:

God is not malicious, but careless, random, extravagant, indiscriminate. I don't base what Faith I have on the feeling of "what a friend I have in Jesus", but on that continual, inescapable sense of the power and the mystery and the danger and profligacy of it all. I mean *all*, from the bizarre goings-on inside each atom—wave function and proton exchange and reverse time—right through to the social complexity of history and class and gender and race and individual experience.

The Church and the Great Novel both try to structure that intellectually and emotionally, both to contain and to reveal it. Form, it is called, form and structure and genre. I cling to orthodoxy in theology and to form in cultural production. The challenge is to go as near to the edge, as near to the power and the mystery and the danger, without collapsing into chaos. We need as many counterweights, as many interrupt factors as we can lay our hands on. Neither the Great Novel nor the Church seems to be working too well at the moment. We just catch the fragments as best we can—but it is all one chaos, I think, though differently delineated, represented. [1988, pp. 167–168, original emphasis]

Nevertheless, a theologian needs to take seriously Freud's criticism of religious and political belief-systems: that they serve to defend the child in us against the terrors of the universe, against the fear of chaos (1933a, p. 162). But Freud is at times in danger of extolling intellect in place of religious belief, without acknowledging, as he does elsewhere, that rationalization is also a form of illusion. The theologian's task is largely intellectual, as there is also an important intellectual aspect to psychotherapy and counselling, even if, more often than not, it is a quiet reflective process that precedes an intervention. Weinstein, in an essay titled "The social function of intellectuals", describes that function in this way:

> [Intellectuals] provide the conceptual language people need to bring order to the complex experiences of everyday life . . . linking past and present in a comprehensive and orderly way, encouraging people thereby to continue to believe in a future consistent with needs and expectations. [1980, p. 3]

Others, of course, also have insights (indeed it is part of the therapeutic process), but the intellectual has the capacity to symbolize thought; this symbolic language is itself therapeutic, providing a sense of order in the midst of chaos.

Weinstein suggests that this task "of ordering ceaseless change and novelty" requires a person to possess a degree of narcissism: an intellectual has to believe in him- or herself. This is necessary to endure the chaos of some stages of thinking. The intellectual needs to believe he or she *can* be correct, and perhaps has to be like a capricious god who wants to make things go her or his way. Yet we are not gods. Tolkien has it right when he describes us as "sub-creators"—even when someone produces something completely original, that person has been influenced by others. Rycroft was right to counter the narcissism of the original thinker with his essay "On ablation of parental images *or* the illusion of having created oneself" (1985, pp. 214–232).

But if a thinker *can* be correct, he or she should not believe he or she *is* correct. As long as it does not become over-inflated, the intellectual needs an inflatable jacket before plunging into the sea of chaos and questioning. Questioning is invariably a lonely task—the thinker becomes engrossed in a turbulent inner world; because that inner world of thought is turbulent, there is something lacking in the experience of those therapists who stress feeling and see thought as mere intellectualization. They appear never to have known the anxieties of the thinker.

The narcissism that is necessary to cope with the chaotic process of thought can lead intellectuals to overreach themselves. Weinstein comments that "even the very best of them are not as correct as they need to think they are". The great thinkers who try to order the chaotic (whether it be the external world like Darwin and Marx or the internal world like Freud and Jung) tend to see themselves as creating a permanent order, mistaking their role as "sub-creators" for the creator. Freud, for instance, wished that he could find evidence through psychoanalysis for the effect of the mind on the body in order to prove the Lamarckian theory of evolution rather than the Darwinian view. He believed that "this would actually supply a psychoanalytic explanation of adaptation; it would put the coping stone on psychoanalysis" (Abraham & Freud, 1965, p. 262). This has the appearance of a phantasy of omnipotence and omni-science, what in the same context Freud calls, even though writing about hysteria, "the omnipotence of thoughts".

Weinstein warns:

> All intellectual constructions, however grand, must be approached with more than a grain of salt. All such constructions are charac-terised by notable weaknesses as well as strengths, with the added difficulty that the weaknesses are often subtly masked because of *the therapeutic and ideological functions.* These weaknesses can then become as important, or even more important, than the strengths because of the need people have for these constructions. Their own force, and the frailties of their followers, can make them as much an obstacle as a spur to further progress in the areas which they do brilliantly pioneer. [1980, p. 3, my emphasis].

If the great intellectuals risk becoming omniscient, it is their less than original followers who are more greatly tempted to elevate the master's thought to an order which cannot be questioned, in an attempt to prevent chaos breaking into their own sense of order. New myths are created from what may be tentative theories. At the same time, we would not have professionals who thought them-selves gods if their patients and clients did not treat them so. We see it happening to political leaders, too, when the masses hand over to them the responsibility for ordering chaos—hence the appeal at times of economic and political stress of simplistic, often extremist, ideologies, whether fascism or communism, monetarism or militancy, fundamentalism or millennarianism. The fallible authority of the thinker is raised above principalities and powers, and the more charismatic the thinker, the greater the risk. Theories are turned into tablets of stone. While there always need to be times of rest and consolidation, too great a sense of having arrived prevents us moving forward, however tempting it is to rest upon one's laurels. Brother William, in *The Name of the Rose*, expresses it this way:

> The order that our mind imagines is like a net, or like a ladder, built to attain something. But afterward you must throw the ladder away, because you discover that, even if it was useful, it was meaningless . . . The only truths that are useful are instruments to be thrown away. [Eco, 1983, p. 492]

This ossification of thought is as apparent in some of Freud's followers as it is in the way religious or ideological institutions have usually developed. Bettelheim (1982) has drawn attention to the ways in which Freud's translators altered much of his meaning through making his work more definitive and quasi-scientific than Freud intended. He gives examples such as the titles of Freud's books. *The Interpretation of Dreams* does not convey Freud's original title, which is better rendered, *A Search for the Meaning of Dreams*. Bettelheim cites the original translators into English employing quasi-scientific terms such as "parapraxis" when Freud's phrase means "faulty achievements"; and the use of "ego" and "id" as impersonal latinate terms, when Freud uses the personal pronouns "I" and "it"—the latter in the sense of "something in me". Even more startling is Bettelheim's observation that Freud constantly uses the German word for "soul" and that his first translators nearly always substitute the word "mind". (This situation has been altered in the more recent publication of new translations of Freud's major works in the Penguin Classics editions, edited by Adam Phillips.) Bettelheim observes that the "emotionally distancing language of the translations" has conveyed the image of psychoanalysis as analysing selected aspects of others, whereas "Freud's insights threaten our narcissistic image of ourselves" (1982, pp. 15–16). Therapy is not a cure-all for mental disorder, but a means of exploring the chaos of the darkest recesses of the soul.

People bring their stories, their myths, and their constructions of reality to therapists because they want to make sense of their chaos. For many, it will only be the experience of entering that chaotic inner world that enables them to be re-created: the client will be the guide as long as the therapist is neither too timid nor too demanding. In such cases they might have only tentative ideas to go upon, a distant light upon the other shore, of which they can lose sight when, like Leander, they enter the Hellespont of the soul. Pursuing this symbol, remembering how ancient near eastern mythology symbolizes chaos as the waters of the deep, therapists know from experience that they will usually beach on the other side, and will then be able to look back with greater clarity to the point from which they and their client departed together. But this is little consolation at the point of wading in, especially when clients clamour for assurance that they will emerge unscathed upon the other side. Therapists, therefore, need not only to be sensitive to how much buffeting or chaos the client can take, but also need that semi-narcissistic faith that convinces them they are right, and that they will not be lost completely in the deep. At the same time they are conscious that when they appear to walk on water (when the cognitive appears so convincing, for instance), there is always the risk of wishful thinking.

The image of the sea in Freud's work stands for the unconscious. In the *New Introductory Lectures* he qualifies the goal of psychoanalysis, variously described as the ego mastering the super-ego, the id and the external world; or "Where id was there shall ego be" (1933a, p. 80), a phrase followed by a powerful image drawn from the Dutch engineers' reclamation of land from the sea: "It is a work of culture—not unlike the draining of the Zuider Zee" (*ibid.*). Bettelheim notes this apt simile. The sea

> is a primordial dominant element of the natural world, comparable to the it in the world of the psyche . . . When the Zuyder Zee project was completed, only a tiny part of the vast North Sea had been pushed back. The project has remained a precarious achievement, because the reclaimed land has to be continuously protected against renewed flooding. A furious onslaught of the elements, such as a huge tidal wave, could undo much of what has been accomplished. The parallels here to the it in relation to the I, and to the work of psychoanalysis, are obvious. [1982, pp. 62–63]

The therapist is aware that there are defences against the creativity of chaos, and that one of the major defences is the wish for order, seen *par excellence* in the authoritarian and the obsessional personality. Such people look for certainty and safety, unable to tolerate doubt and confusion, fearful of the dark side of themselves. They wish the therapist to provide structure, orders, advice, and reassurance, and elevate the therapist to oracular status.

This defence of idealism in the client, or the glowing optimism of the therapist, masks the recognition of the unpleasant, the dark, the bad, the evil, the shadow—whatever we choose to call that "negative" side in human life. The wise never underestimate the force of the sea. Those therapists who take the negative seriously, such as Freud, Jung, and Klein, reared as they were in European tradition of angst and not in the frequently false optimism of the New World, hold together the tension between good experience and bad experience, good and bad breast, God and Satan, which can never be neatly ordered. Bettelheim casts this in terms of the two underlying principles of Freud's later theory:

> For Freud the I was a sphere of tragic conflict. From the moment we are born until the moment we die, Eros and Thanatos struggle for dominance in shaping our lives, and make it difficult for us to be at peace with ourselves for anything but short periods. It is this struggle which makes emotional richness possible; which explains the multifarious nature of a man's life; which makes alike for depression and elation; which gives life its deepest meaning. [*ibid.*, p. 109]

The multifarious nature of life is not just the lot of *homo sapiens*, but extends to the whole of creation. It is not the thinker's objective to tame that multifariousness, but to embrace it in every discipline. Even science, assumed by so many non-scientists to be the epitome of order, can only put constructions upon experience, upon what is mistakenly called the "natural order", because the natural order is constantly being shaken, not only by new research, but in its very essence. Although we look for, and indeed find, symmetry in the atom or the cosmos, the random phenomenon, like the random thought, alters the balance of creation, pushing it back into what might be called microcosmic chaos, out of which new forms emerge. The variety of organic life is the result of the random gene, of random mutations. Nothing is ever fixed. It has been the strength of theology, especially when it was seen as the Queen of the Sciences, that as a discipline it looks not simply at what is happening in the here and now to humanity alone, but at the totality of the cosmos and of immeasurable time, and is aware of continuous flux, like the sea itself. With the questioning of the driving force of theology, the nature of God, nothing quite like that discipline has taken its place in secular culture.

The therapist may be able to help people to enter the chaotic elements of their past in order to re-evaluate the present, but can never protect anyone from the randomness of the future (see also Chapter Nine on Fate). However careful the choices we make, and whatever constructions we put upon experience to tolerate and contain it, the random will always threaten equilibrium, and sometimes brings chaos. The greatest help a therapist can be is to enable a person to find a strong enough sense of self to face the chaos of the future, to hold together in its midst, and to believe that it can engender creativity. We only do that by taking chaos seriously, not by wishing it away through illusory belief that all will be well, and all will end "happily ever after".

I have referred in this chapter to the story-teller, the novelist and dramatist, the thinker, the scientist, the theologian, and the therapist, and have suggested one of the bonds that is common to them. Conrad writes in the Preface to *The Nigger of the Narcissus*:

> Impressed by the aspect of the world the thinker plunges into ideas, the scientist into facts whence, presently, emerging they make their appeal to those qualities of our being that fit us best for the hazardous enterprise of living. They speak authoritatively to our common sense, to our intelligence, to our desire for peace or to *our desire of unrest*. Confronted by the same enigmatic spectacle the artist descends within himself and in that lonely region of stress and strife, he finds the terms of his appeal. [1963, p. 11, my emphasis]

I have arrived, at least for this moment, at a destination that I vaguely glimpsed when I started to think about "our desire of unrest". I found myself at the start feeling like Tolkien at that point in writing *The Lord of the Rings* when he broke off to write his essay on faerie:

> At that time we had reached Bree, and I then had no more notion than they had of what had become of Gandalf or who Strider was; and I had begun to despair of surviving to find out. [1964, p. 5]

Or perhaps I was like the therapist who does not know what areas of understanding or confusion each new client will bring. Or like the theologian, who loses a heartbeat at the thought that God, whose work has at times paid a comfortable wage, does not exist.

If I have communicated my random thoughts clearly enough, the reader will be able to affirm the necessity of chaos. My anxiety, if I am to remain true to what I write, is lest this ordering is seen as complete in itself, because then I shall have failed to encourage the reader to follow the thinking through. If we delude ourselves at any point that we have "got it made", we shall have lost the very stuff of creation.

CHAPTER THREE

Naming and labelling

My first journal publication, which led to other invitations to write, appeared in 1976, in the journal *Contact*, which addressed the interface between pastoral care and counselling and disciplines such as the social sciences, psychology, and theology. I represented the then Association of Pastoral Care and Counselling on the journal's editorial board. I was working at that time in the Student Health service at the University of Leicester, where I was the sole therapist. My colleagues were doctors who, for the most part, were psychologically minded, and not usually as those described in this article. Nevertheless, the experience of being immersed in the medical world, and engaging in conversations which certainly did include technical terms that were sometimes foreign to me, no doubt forced me to think about the whole diagnostic process in medicine, and how it related to the work I was doing with the clients referred to me by the medical staff. It was, in one sense, not a very original idea, and I was soon to discover that there was plenty of criticism of the psychiatric medical model even within psychiatry itself. However, the concept of naming, which features in the second half of the chapter, was a more original idea, and it is that part of the original paper that I later expanded when asked to talk about the subject. Byatt's writing made a particular impression on me; and that part of the paper also formed a significant section of the second chapter of my book *The Presenting Past* (2006). Much has changed since the paper was first written— with many more general practices, or primary care as it is now known, including counsellors in the team. This has influenced my revision of the paper for publication here, although I suspect that some of the issues I raise in the first half are as relevant to those counsellors in their relationships with medical staff as they were for me when I started my career in counselling and psychotherapy.

*   *   *

Those who work as therapists and counsellors in a setting such as primary care often find themselves alongside other professionals for whom clarity of purpose and precision in diagnosis is important, and whose working conversation sometimes appears filled with terms that would certainly justify the expression "It's all Greek to me". Those who have not initially trained in medicine, nursing, or even psychology can feel uncomfortable, not simply because they are spoken to in what seems a special language that they do not always understand, but also because of their unease with the way patients (or clients as they may prefer to say) are talked about. Indeed, for some therapists, to use the term "patient" suggests a medical model, one which increases the dependency of "the patient" upon the expert, or appears to make people into machines in which parts have gone wrong, or malfunctioning systems that need a service. And, although it is particularly true of the medical profession, it is also present in other caring situations that patients or clients, or their symptoms and problems, have all the appearance of being labelled. There is a stronger tradition among counsellors to see people as persons, rather than cases, and for their work, whatever their orientation, to be person-centred. (It is not necessary to be a Rogerian to be person-centred.) Working in a medical setting in particular might well feel disturbing when people and problems are referred to and understood in less personal ways, even when professional colleagues treat those they see with respect and care and give them the very best of their expertise.

Technical and impersonal language is also seen in the vocabulary that is used at the more advanced levels of training that many psychotherapists have undertaken. Therapists and counsellors, particularly those beginning their training, whose preoccupation when with clients is not with books and theories, but with the words and feelings of those who seek their help, might at times experience their own descriptions, attitudes, and feelings as amateurish and simplistic; yet in their communication with colleagues in the medical or psychotherapy setting, they may feel obliged to use a technical vocabulary and diagnostic categories as if they were bread-and-butter terms. When others are using words such as "borderline personality", "psychotic", "neurotic", "character disorder", "bi-polar disorder", "obsessional", or "hysteric" with such frequency as the rest of us use prepositions and conjunctions, those who are wanting to prove their value as counsellors and demonstrate their expertise as therapists do not simply have to learn to understand these terms; they might feel under pressure to adopt them.

Labelling is also found in a rather different setting. I draw in this chapter upon some aspects of the religious tradition, particularly middle-eastern thinking. Organized religion has an equally technical terminology, which frequently makes those not conversant with it truly feel outside the fold. More than that, religious institutions have often used terminology to divide and denigrate, giving rise to the most negative form of labelling, one that identifies and distinguishes behaviour and belief as that which is acceptable and that which is unacceptable. Labels, such as Catholic and Protestant, Christian and Jew and Muslim, or fundamentalist and radical, have often foreclosed the possibility of constructive debate. The tendency to label and to place people in different camps, and in so doing to make value judgements about them, has its parallel in counselling and psychotherapy with the many different divisions (what in religious terms are called "sects") within that area of discourse. Indeed, it is sometimes seen in the way some people like to make clear divisions between those who are labelled counsellors, those who are called psychotherapists, and those who wish to adopt the label psychoanalyst. (Regulation of the psychotherapy and counselling professions in the UK makes this question of labelling even more relevant.) Although I concentrate here upon naming and labelling as it applies to clinical work, it is important not to forget the way labelling is used and misused within these different professions themselves.

Categorization, which labelling to some extent represents, is, of course, an inevitable part of every intellectual discipline. I am not alone in having doubts about the value of the type of research that leads to false categorization and to over-simplification. Counselling and psychotherapy sometimes feels less than empirical and less scientific because it is not usually backed up by statistics and quantifiable results. (Most counselling and psychotherapy research is, of course, qualitative, which, if now more acceptable than once it was, is none the less more impressionistic.) Statistical methods have their weakness. I remember many years ago being asked to complete a questionnaire on student counselling in which I was asked to list the prevalence of a dozen presenting problems. Not only were a number of important of areas of personal distress omitted, but there seemed to be little recognition that the majority of people present a number of issues that are obviously linked, and that such presenting problems are only the top layer of complex issues that nothing short of a paragraph could describe. Around that time, in my own effort to research my own work, I attempted to analyse data from 190 case histories so as initially to identify the major presenting problems. There were 132 different presentations, and, in most instances, more than one person experiencing each one. So, although it might have been reasonable for me to say that thirty-five per cent of that sample presented some degree of depression, or twenty-five per cent of them had problems with relationships, there was not much more that could usefully be said between such a generalized analysis on the one hand, and on the other that there were 190 very different presentations. Obviously, empirical study does not have to rely solely on statistics and number crunching, but it frequently has to narrowly define the area of research, and as a result presents a misleading impression of what is really involved in the work and how complex most people's lives are.

I do not intend to propose an isolationist stance, one which eschews the value of categorization and research, even though I am less interested in it than I am in the person who is sitting with me, each of us concerned more for individual circumstances than the way others are, or the way other therapists work. Nor do I wish to denigrate the use of technical language—as long as it is primarily intended as shorthand that enables those working in a particular professional setting to communicate more clearly and precisely with each other. I recognize, as one who has written much, that communication can only take place through the use of language, and that some languages are inevitably more complex than others. We all need language, including technical language, to make intelligent use of the knowledge and expertise enshrined in such terms in the relevant literature. I do, however, want to challenge some of the assumptions that go with the use of categories, labels, and technical language. I do want to indicate some of its limitations. And, more significantly, I want to propose a more relevant and effective way of understanding and using the process of identifying what troubles people, which is as much a part of professional training and practice.

First, it is important to recognize that even where technical language and labelling represent definite symptoms and syndromes and their possible causes, what the professional perceives, and sometimes what the client chooses to present, can vary from person to person and from interview to interview. Those counsellors and therapists who have ever looked at case notes, particularly of people who have seen several consultants, doctors, or psychologists, will be aware of way in which such patients are often placed in a variety of diagnostic categories. Examples come to light that turn what appears to be a neat system of categorization into one of real confusion: one client, whose notes I referred, had even been diagnosed in four different ways by the same psychiatrist in four different letters to the GP!

Before we let such examples undermine our simple faith in the knowledge of the experts, there are explanations for the confusion that appears to be present in the diagnostic process. The "experts" might, of course, themselves perceive the same symptoms differently and therefore disagree in their diagnosis. Apart from sometimes significant differences in diagnosis from one culture to another, there are also important shifts even in short time spans— the prime example being homosexuality, once a diagnostic category in psychiatry. Schizophrenia, or the types of behaviour which lead to various labels connected with severe mental disturbance, also vary, not just from culture to culture, but also within psychiatry itself. Furthermore, there are fashions in medicine and in psychiatry. A GP I worked with observed the changing fashions of the years. At one time his patients came back from consultants with a note suggesting a prescription for Valium or Librium. "Now," he said somewhat cynically, "they are all coming back with a note saying that they have a personality problem, as if I am expected to know what to do about that!" Fashions in matters psychological and psychiatric are, none the less, as much fads as in any other profession, although I suspect that they are rather more, and an indication of the vast gaps in knowledge that inevitably still exist, which experts often disguise since they (the consultants) are expected to be wise.

But it is not just the experts who can be contrary-wise. Clients can present different aspects or sides of themselves, depending upon the mood that is uppermost in them on the day of their consultation. There is also the psychological defence (inevitably, I, too, have to use a technical term to summarize it) known as splitting: a phenomenon where clients need to keep parts of themselves separate from each other within themselves, as much as they separate their symptoms in speaking to different people. They might, therefore, present only part of the picture to one person, and sometimes different parts to different persons, because of their need to keep them apart within themselves. Then there is a third explanation, which lies neither exclusively with the professional nor with the client, but in the relationship between them. It is a phenomenon that is just as evident in counselling and therapy: the client's presentation of symptoms is adapted to, or partly takes its expression from, the relationship between the counsellor and the client. Not only do clients learn to speak what they think their therapists want to hear (and vice versa), the way they present themselves and their issues is also a way of speaking about the current therapeutic relationship. A simple example might be the client who, when asked what brings her for therapy, begins by saying that she feels very anxious. Her anxiety might not the symptom that she originally wanted to talk about: it is the expression of how she feels about seeing the therapist. Of course, this may be linked with other experiences in her life, but what medicine defines as the iatrogenic factor (that caused by the doctor) cannot be ignored. Freud, of course, recognized it as the transference neurosis. Most therapists

encountering this example would not make the mistake of identifying the client's specific anxiety as the actual presenting problem,
but in more complex presentations anyone could make such an
error.

I have already indicated that I recognize the necessity and value
of a certain amount of labelling, particularly when it is done with a
careful eye to accuracy. The psychological aspects of a doctor's
work, for example, can benefit from the extension of the systematic
method of history-taking, examination, assessment/diagnosis, and
treatment. In this context, a certain amount of labelling is inevitable.
Obviously, when prescribing, the doctor wishes to find the right
diagnosis and the diagnosis naturally becomes a label. Not all
doctors and psychiatrists hand out drugs indiscriminately, and the
doctor who believes in the efficacy of psychotropic treatment will
want to select the right drug, and therefore want to make an accurate diagnosis. He or she will often recognize that there is no clear
line to be drawn between, let us say, an anxiety state and depression, and this is indeed reflected in what the doctor can prescribe,
such as an anti-depressant that also contains an anti-anxiolytic.
Nevertheless, the need to label can also lead to stretching labels
beyond recognition. One such instance I encountered through
supervision of a therapist, whose client's psychiatrist had labelled
her an "atypical bulimic". In fact, she only occasionally ate too
much, and then might take laxatives. But it was not a major part of
her presenting problem, and, as I said to the therapist discussing
her, you might just as well call me an "atypical schizophrenic"!

Yet effective labelling may also help the patient, especially when
the presentation is physical. It is reassuring to consult a GP with,
for example, a pain in the chest, and to be told that your own feared
labelling of the pain as cancer, bronchitis, or heart trouble is not
right, and to be given a different, much more reassuring label: that
you have, for instance, strained a muscle while painting a high ceil-
ing. And if the cause of the pain were more serious, it is probably
not only the GP, but also the patient, who would want a definite
label to be attached as soon as possible. Even if the prognosis looks
unfavourable, the naming of the illness has a particular kind of
reassurance for the patient—usually it is better, though not less
painful, to know rather than to be kept in the dark, although much
depends upon the way the news is communicated. Although these

matters are clearly more complex than I can do justice to here, knowing is generally more conducive to health than not-knowing. The different outcomes of such labelling can be seen clearly if a person having difficulty reading is labelled as dyslexic. This can be a relief; but on the other hand being labelled epileptic, which immediately brings restrictions, might not be. If the label then becomes the identity of the person, as sometimes happens when health care professionals or people generally talk of "an epileptic", rather than an epileptic person, or as a geriatric, rather than a geriatric person, this is not only depersonalizing, as an adjective is turned into a noun, but the noun appears to indicate what is substantive, what is the core of the person, whereas the adjectival form is only one way of describing a person, which in many circumstances can be set to one side.

Nevertheless, in a busy surgery, some labelling forecloses a person's attempt to reveal deeper anxieties. The doctor might well provide a quick and a slick answer, including well meant reassurance. He or she will probably not have the time to explore, for example, the *meaning* of a person's fear of what a pain in the chest signifies, even when that person already half knew that it might be something like a strained muscle. And when attempting to describe psychological states, there is rather more doubt about the value of the label. The patient who bursts into tears, says he cannot sleep or concentrate upon his work, and is told that he is suffering from depression might feel temporarily relieved (and indeed some people do), but in fact they are only being told the obvious. There might, however, be some assurance even in the obvious when it comes from the expert. Such labelling may help relieve some of the distress, especially if the label is of a condition that many others also suffer from, or relates to an emotional state that is to be expected—such as the feelings that follow a bereavement. (Although even then some doctors seem to think such feelings merit a prescription, thus pathologizing them.) However, some who are told they are depressed or suffer from an anxiety state can inflate such a label into a fear that they are going mad or having a breakdown.

A doctor's calm manner, and their labelling of what is wrong, can lessen such fear: a diagnosis, even if it is not strictly accurate, or even if it is tautologous (that is, saying what the patient has said, but in rather grander language) can have the effect of providing a sense of order for patients whose confusion otherwise is likely to increase their anxiety. Labelling can provide a measure of security, although it is often only temporary (which is why quite a number are back in the surgery the following week). Indeed, the label is less likely to satisfy when the patient is not only asking what is wrong, but also wants to know why. Such questions normally take longer to answer than is permitted by the very brief time that the average GP can give in surgery hours. That is a good point for referral for counselling, where there could be an opportunity to allow deeper expression and the possible revelation of personal difficulties (although limits on the number of sessions available makes this a careful task for the counsellor).

If the psychological effect of the label is important for a patient or client, might labelling also be psychologically helpful for a doctor or a nurse, or even for a counsellor? I have already acknowledged that medical education and training gears the doctor or nurse to making a diagnosis, and from that to forming a treatment plan. Labelling is a necessary step in a sequence of steps, which may result, as far as the GP is concerned, in a prescription, or a word of advice, or in a referral letter to see either a consultant or a counsellor. Yet, if this is an obvious way in which labelling helps the doctor and the person to whom referral is made, there is more to it than that. In the hierarchy of consultant, GP, nurse, and counsellor it is perhaps as important for the counsellor, in particular, to feel that he or she can do something which will impress the GP as it is for the counsellor to wish to help the patient. While labelling is a way of improving communication within the medical profession, it also might be used to show that the counsellor is doing something, not just listening (even if just listening may actually be the most effective treatment). Yet, I have examples of where a label appears to have been a way of fobbing off patients: one client was referred by his GP to a psychiatrist because the client had marital problems. Here was medical obscurantism at its best, because the psychiatrist told the man and the referring GP that the cause of the marital problems was his premature ejaculation. Fortunately, the client had enough sense to know that the cause of his premature ejaculation was his marital situation, and that his problems would not be solved by concentrating upon this one symptom.

It is easy, of course, to knock experts and to claim the higher ground when they cannot fulfil our idealistic fantasies of them. Those of us whose work concentrates upon a person's inner world, with all its emotions and internal objects, are all too aware that this is an area that abounds with confusion and contradiction and that it is full of intense and often disturbing feelings, for clients as well as for therapists. Labelling sometimes provides an important sense of security, a reference point in the midst of bewilderment, upon which we can fasten and from which we can move. Particularly where the label is not a simple catch-phrase, but represents a more complex network of linked symptoms and problems, and of potential aetiology, it can also provide a range of possible clues to look out for in the material with which the therapist is presented. The label "depression", for instance, is of little use in itself, but leads to looking further, since there are many variations as to what the depression expresses, let alone to the immediate cause: it can be from a sense of loss, or a result of guilt, or self-loathing, or repressed anger, an over-zealous conscience, a morally or physically punitive upbringing, or any combination of such and other factors. The label then becomes a means not of closing off the issue, or of impressing the client with knowledge, but of widening the horizon and of triggering off a series of associations and questions that can extend the therapeutic plan. Similarly, where there is useful labelling evident in previous notes, or in letters of referral, counsellors and therapists can benefit from other people's perceptions before they develop, with the patient, their own treatment plans. Some of the labels that others have used, as long as they are not taken as infallible, may also provide warning signals, just as the labels that some patients present about themselves can suggest caution to the counsellor and alert him or her to contra-indications for a particular approach or particular skills.

There is, therefore, some value in labelling, even for the counsellor, and therefore in learning both the language and the method that the medical setting often uses, since, used well, it can benefit both the professional and the client. But the idea of identifying what is wrong is capable of a much richer way of working and of understanding than the use of labelling generally permits. I want, therefore, to introduce a second term, which encapsulates a different concept and a different attitude in the therapist: this aspect I call "naming". Although this might, in some circumstances, prove to be interchangeable with the term "labelling", it has a distinctive meaning, one that can be illustrated particularly from a middle-eastern cultural and religious context, but which also applies outside that discourse.

This might be illustrated in the way the different concepts of labelling and naming were used in an interchange with a client who had seen me for quite a long time. One day she asked me what I would say was wrong with her. "Am I a manic-depressive, am I neurotic, do I have an anxiety state?" she asked. I was not at all sure which of these she would want me to identify, if any. And I said, truthfully but with some trepidation about her likely response, that I was generally not interested in attaching those kind of labels to people. To my relief, she replied that if I did, she would want a category all to herself! The reason was obvious: she came from a large family, in which she was the very middle child; time and again she had talked of situations both in her family and in present relationships where she felt that she did not matter. She saw herself as always left out of invitations to parties, she felt people ignored her, she recalled how her parents had teased her when she showed early signs of intellectual promise, which marked her out from their other children. She desperately wanted recognition, and yet she also felt guilty when she got it. She wanted to be treated as a unique individual. And she was prepared, had I labelled her, to insist on that too in any "diagnosis".

It is the uniqueness of the individual that lies behind the ancient concept of "naming". Ursula Le Guin, in her fantasy novel *A Wizard of Earthsea* (1971), employs this concept in a remarkably powerful way. Although each person, each animate object and each inanimate object, has a common name, one which is used in normal speech, each also has a special and secret name. In the case of animals and objects this name has been passed down from ancient times in ancient speech. People are given their true name either in infancy or at puberty.

Salman Rushdie employs a similar concept, in his case clearly a Muslim one, in his novel *Haroun and the Sea of Stories*. In one episode the Water Genie asks Haroun to pick a bird to travel upon. Haroun looks around the room but only sees a peacock carved in wood. The Water Genie tells Haroun that he can choose what he cannot see.

A person may mention a bird's name even if the creature is not present and correct . . . A person may even select a flying creature of his own invention . . . To give a thing a name, a label, a handle; to rescue it from anonymity, to pluck it out of the Place of Name- lessness, in short to identify it—well, that's a way of bringing the said thing into being. [Rushdie, 1990, p. 63]

There is a positive and a negative side to this concept. Haroun clearly benefits when he can name his means of flying, but, by the same token, naming may bring the more feared imaginations into being. I return to this point below. Naming is an awesome act, and this is seen in the way in which Ursula Le Guin develops her story. She observes that those who are wise are able to control objects and people only when they are able to give them their true name. Because of the power of the name, people give their true name only to those whom they can trust. "A man never speaks his own name aloud, until more than his life's safety is at stake" (Le Guin, 1971, p. 46). The giving of your name to the other gives the other a certain power over you. Such a fictional concept is shown to have a real basis in some cultures, particularly in the East and the Middle East. In his book on psychology and religion, Leslie Weatherhead simi- larly writes about the significance of a person's name. He describes how, in the East, giving one's name is felt to be the surrender of power to another (1963, p. 64). I experienced the same power of the name when in Egypt. Some of the traders in the bazaar were eager to find out my name, and once they had learned it, used it constantly in their sales pitch and their bartering. It had a powerful effect, and I learned to avoid both giving my name and, in some instances, establishing eye contact, each of which easily became an opening for a quite invasive process.

Weatherhead observes that there were a number of Indians in a regiment in which he served who would not give their true name lest their officers should acquire an uncanny power over them. In case of their death, they kept their true name in a little cylinder on their person. Similarly, he says an Indian bride would not give her true name to her bridegroom until after the marriage ceremony. Weatherhead is particularly interested in the way these examples reflect the significance of naming in the Judaeo-Christian tradition. He cites the episode in the Old Testament where the angel wrestles with Jacob and asks Jacob his name. Jacob gives it, but when he asks the angel his name, none is given (Genesis, 32: 24–30). Similarly, the power of the name is seen in the New Testament, for example in Christ's healing of the man possessed by many devils. It does not matter for our purposes whether this story is true or not. What is crucial in that story is the question "What is your name?" and the devils' reply "Our name is Legion", which gives Christ power over them (Mark, 5: 9).

The power involved in the act of naming is the central feature of Le Guin's story *A Wizard of Earthsea*. The story is of a young hero, Sparrowhawk, who, in a fit of youthful pride, conjures up a shadow from the dead, which nearly destroys him. The shadow follows him and he tries to flee from it, without success. An old wizard, the one who had given Sparrowhawk his true name, tells him that he must stop running, turn and face the shadow, and name it. Sparrowhawk protests, "The evil thing, the shadow that hunts me, has no name." "*All* things have a name" is the reply. Sparrowhawk turns and now becomes the pursuer, while the shadow becomes the pursued, until at the ends of the earth he names it. Without revealing the climax of the story, there is enough in this description to provide a glimpse of the relevance of this concept for therapy and counselling.

Naming can be seen to form an important part of the therapeutic process—far more important than labelling. First, it is an essential part of the initial sessions where a client is given the space to name what it is that is troubling her or him. This process not only brings inner distress into the open, but it also begins, although it only begins, the process of removing the fear and anxiety aroused by and associated with such feelings. Naming starts the process of owning and controlling the person's fear of inner experiences. Second, naming is seen in the therapist's response in recognizing the individuality of the person, treating the client not as "another depressive", but as a unique individual, with her or his own particular problems, and her or his own life experience contributing to those problems. Third, whether the therapeutic relationship is a brief or a long one, it provides the opportunity of naming those parts of the self which frighten the individual, so that in the ongoing process of naming, as in the initial naming of what troubles them, the client experiences considerable easing of the power that those aspects have over the self. Such naming takes place in a variety of ways. Parts of the body and bodily functions, for instance, given their proper name by therapist and client, can be rescued from their association with guilt and shame—particularly the erotogenic areas of the body. Then, even if there is now much more freedom of expression than forty years or more ago, there are terms like "gay" for some, "masturbation" for others, which, when named, cease to be hold the same power over an individual's possible sense of shame. Similarly, other aspects, particularly some emotional responses or "forbidden" feelings like hate, jealousy, revenge, envy, even, perhaps for some people, love, when they can be named come within the compass of an individual's sensed of ownership, rather than being repressed or suppressed. Anxiety and guilt about feelings, actions, thoughts, parts of the mind and parts of the body are lessened as each can be named and brought into the open.

However, this is a subtle process. It is not enough, any more than it is enough with simple labelling, for a therapist to hammer a client into submissive acceptance by her or his own language or by technical interpretation. Naming takes place when something that is already known by the client is given that final push into consciousness or into words.

In a very different type of novel to the fantasy novels cited above, A. S. Byatt writes of the recognition that takes place when we see something that, even at the point of seeing, we realize was always there.

> Now and then there are readings which make the hairs on the neck, the non-existent pelt, stand upon end and tremble, when every word burns and shines hard and clear and infinite and exact, like stones of fire, like points of stars in the dark—readings when the knowledge that we *shall know* the writing differently or better or satisfactorily, runs ahead of any capacity to say what we know or how. In these readings, a sense that the text has appeared to be wholly new, never before seen, is followed almost immediately, by the sense that it was *always* there, that we the readers, knew that it was always there, and have *always known* it was as it was, though we have now for the first time recognised, become fully cognisant of, our knowledge. [1990, pp. 471–472; original italics]

There is no magic, no secret formula, no clever interpretation that can reach that depth of a person unless that person is already near to self-recognition. "A mage can control only what is near him, what he can name exactly and wholly" (Le Guin, 1971, p. 60). A therapist speaks only of what is known (how can he or she presume to do otherwise?), not from a theoretical background, however much theory may inform their listening. Theory sometimes proves to be true, and sometimes proves not to be true. Unless it is translated into an individual's current presentation, it is likely to give rise to interpretations that make the therapist feel more secure than the client. Naming on the basis of theory alone may give the counsellor the feeling of doing something, but it probably also colludes with the magical phantasy that as an expert the counsellor has only to "speak the word" (Matthew, 8: 8) and the client will be healed. Interpretation, especially if it is based on guesswork and not what the therapist "can name exactly and wholly" (Le Guin, 1971, p. 60) may even give a therapist the sort of power over the client that the person most fears. It is vital, when naming takes place, whether by therapist or client, that power should remain with the client, and that power should be based on self-recognition. Therapists must not replace repression or suppression with oppression.

It is instructive to find that Freud also wrote about the need to get close to what the client is trying to express, rather than interpreting indiscriminately. In one of his papers on technique he warned against the analyst imposing ideas upon the patient. "It is not difficult for a skilled analyst to read the patient's secret wishes plainly between the lines of his complaints and the story of his illness" (1913c, p. 140). But he stressed the danger of plunging in with interpretations when the patient is a "stranger", adding that

> even in the later stages of analysis one must be careful not to give
> a patient the solution of a symptom or a translation of a wish until
> he is already so close to it that he has only one short step more to
> make in order to get hold of the explanation for himself. [*ibid.*]

What Freud demonstrates in some of his case histories is that there is a very thin line between naming at just the right moment, and pressuring a patient or client into accepting the analyst's explanation. Elizabeth von R., for example, complained that Freud's explanation of her pain was not true, that (as Freud put it) "I had talked her into it" (1895d, p. 157). Although Freud appears to have taken care to reassure her in her distress, he does appear to have

forced upon her his recognition of her unconscious wish for a relationship with her brother-in-law. We might wonder whether or not
he was not referring to similar occasions when, in his paper on technique, he acknowledges his own mistakes.

> In former years I often had occasion to find that the premature
> communication of a solution brought the treatment to an untimely
> end, on account not only of the resistances which it thus suddenly
> awakened but also of the relief which the solution brought with it.
> [1913c, pp. 140–141]

Freud appears to have forgotten this in one of his very last papers,
where he asserts that the patient or client is always able to reject the
wrong construction, and that no harm will be done if the analyst
makes a mistake. He adds that if the analyst realizes that a mistake
had been made "we shall admit as much to the patient at some suitable opportunity without sacrificing any of our authority" (1937d,
pp. 261–262). But there is a false optimism about him when Freud
says in the same paper that "an analyst would have had to behave
very incorrectly" (*ibid.*, p. 262) before the danger arose of leading
the patient astray by suggestion. He also appears blind to his
former admission of error when he adds, "I can assert without
boasting that such an abuse of 'suggestion' has never occurred in
my practice" (1937d, p. 262).

What Freud fails to do in this paper, written only a few years
before his death, is to recognize just how powerful the authority of
the analyst or the therapist can be, particularly where the process of
naming is involved. The description of naming that Rushdie's
Water Genie gives Haroun contains an implicit notion that *anything*
can be created by naming it: "A person may even select a flying
creature of his own invention . . . in short to identify it—well, that's
a way of bringing the said thing into being" (1990, p. 63). There are
not a few people who have been damaged by carrying around with
them a psychiatric label that some tactless doctor or psychologist
has given them in the past—the correctness or not of the initial label
is immaterial. And if naming, as I am suggesting, is therapeutically
so much more powerful than labelling, then wrongly used it is by
the same token more dangerous. It is not difficult to see how a therapist can create in a client what might indeed have been dimly part

of the client's unconscious, but which should have been allowed to remain there, by being strictly contained within the boundaries of the therapist's imagination. In his old age, Freud fails to recognize the ability to misuse the power of the interpretation.

Another aging man, a very knowledgeable but largely self-taught naturalist, once spoke to me about what he called "sweet power". This is not power over others, or in the context in which he was speaking, power over our environment. "Sweet power" comes from being able to stand at a particular point in the environment, and looking around, naming the geographical and natural features, being able to recognize the plant and animal life, and the relationship of the parts—including the observer—to the whole in that tiny section of the natural world. It is perhaps something like the naming of the beasts in the Genesis story of creation (Genesis 2: 19–20). It is not merely a scientific exercise, nor (he made it quite clear) is it a way of showing off your knowledge—as I suspect some labelling is. It is a process whereby you feel in touch with, and in tune with, the environment of which you are but one part. Ursula Le Guin makes the old wizard in Earthsea say the same:

> "When you know the fourfoil in all its seasons, root and leaf and flower, by sight and scent and seed, then you may learn its true name, knowing its being; which is more than its use. What, after all, is the use of you? or myself?" Ogon went on a half-mile or so, and said at last, "To hear, one must be silent." The boy frowned . . . kept back his resentment and impatience . . . For he hungered to learn, to gain power. [1971, p. 29]

There is one final aspect of "naming" that also needs recognition. I refer above to the Genesis story of creation, and the power given to Adam to name the creatures. In naming them, Adam was not himself the creator, but was given through naming a share of power over creation (as Chapter Two referred to as well, with Tolkein's term "sub-creator", see p. 21). In one of the poems in her novel *Possession*, Byatt alludes to the Genesis story, echoing in her own way the power of naming that Rushdie and Le Guin also describe:

> The first men named this place and named the world.
> They made the words for it: garden and tree

> Dragon or snake and woman, grass and gold
> And apples. They made names and poetry.
> The things *were* what they named and made them . . .

The significant words follow:

> . . . Next
> They mixed the names and made a metaphor
> Or truth, or visible truth, apples of gold.
> The golden apples brought a rush of words
> The silvery water and the horrent scales
> Upon the serpentining beast, the leaves
> All green and shining on the curving boughs
> (The serpentining boughs) that called to mind
> The lovely gestures of the woman's arms
> Her curving arms, her serpentining arms . . . [1990, p. 464]

In this beautiful playing with words, Byatt reminds us that even "naming" (and, indeed, "labelling") is itself a metaphor, and that all language is a means of trying to bridge the gap between inner experience and outer reality. In describing naming, I express it through words, and most therapists also only use words (arts therapists, of course, have other means whereby their clients can express themselves). This means that what therapists and clients, and writers, indeed, identify and name is still only an approximation to inner experience. Counselling and therapy is full of metaphor, which is why it is an art more than a science, although science also sometimes uses metaphors. If it is more therapeutic to go beyond labelling to naming, it needs to be made clear, as in some instances therapists may find it important to make clear to their clients, that what we speak and what we name might be better than a label, and might carry more force and feeling than a label, but that it is still only a fallible and one dimensional expression of the inner world.

Given this important proviso about language and the power of words, the conclusion of this playing with naming and labelling is that labelling may give the illusion of power, security in the confusion of the inner world, and confidence, particularly in learning about therapy, and in the initial experience of unfamiliar settings. It may enable a degree of clearer communication to take place between the practitioners of a particular set of theory and skills (as long as they know they speak the same language). But labelling runs the risk of merely exercising power, sometimes with colleagues but, more dangerously, power over clients: power to tell them what is wrong, or what they are like, and there is always the risk inherent in any categorization of losing sight of the individual. Naming, on the other hand, ultimately provides deeper security to clients, for in the end they are helped to do the naming themselves. Naming gives them a sense of control that is based less on head knowledge and more on insight and on the acceptance of the more hidden parts of the self. Naming recognizes and explores the "being" and the uniqueness of each individual, for ultimately it is by name we are known, not by label. And if it can be recognized how even naming itself is a metaphor and that what we name are also metaphors, then we are less tempted as therapists to use our knowledge to become as gods (Genesis 3: 5).

CHAPTER FOUR

Optimism and pessimism

This chapter is based on a lecture first given to a day school on the theme "Optimism and pessimism: good and evil" at Vaughan College, Leicester, in 1979. It was subsequently published as an occasional paper by the British Association for Counselling, as it was known then. Although I do not quote from his book, I found Holbrook's *Human Hope and the Death Instinct* (1971) a mine of valuable references which indicated further reading that I do cite below. The theme is still relevant today, since practice-based evidence is demanded by funders deciding whether a particular therapeutic approach is effective. Does it enable change? There is, however, a prior question, and that is whether people can change, and how deep is that change. How might we understand human nature? As this chapter illustrates, such a question divides modalities.

Unlike some of the other papers in this book, the lecture was only given once, and not repeated with necessary revisions at a later date. Preparing it for publication, I have been aware of its length and its attempt to cover too much. Such optimism! This chapter is, therefore, much adapted from the original, in as much as I could do this while still remaining true to opinions that I held then and still hold now. There have been cuts, and a few additions that reflect changes in my thinking.

* * *

The history of humankind reflects a search for understanding and hope in an environment that, for most people at most times, has itself forced upon them the necessity of making sense of external and internal threats. In primitive society, ritual and magic provided a secure framework; in more highly developed societies various forms of religion, philosophy, or political beliefs have attempted to analyse what is wrong with people and society and point forward to a vision of the future. Some have been optimistic and some pessimistic about the state of humankind, although nearly all have held out hope at least for the enlightened followers of a particular system. History has thrown up many salvific movements, charismatic leaders, and promising ideas, which have captured the imagination of some people only to be overthrown or revised radically in later generations. We might sympathize with D. H. Lawrence's plea:

> When wilt thou teach the people,
> God of justice, to save themselves—?
> They have been saved so often
> and sold.
> O God of justice, send no more saviours
> of the people! [1960, p. 143]

A deep concern of mine, shared by critics outside the psychotherapy world, is whether the current therapy and counselling movement could become yet another in a long line of discredited salvific systems. It is tempting to see psychotherapy and counselling as a new hope in an age of increasing bewilderment and despair. I observe below, as others have done, the way in which the psychoanalytic movement was felt to be the answer in its earliest days, particularly among Freud's followers, and how, indeed, it has been regarded since by people at large, noticeably in the fashion for analysis that has pervaded the American way of life. Counselling, which by and large can be traced back by one route or another to the analytic movement, whatever its origin and practice, is always open to idealization, and its various "sects" open to becoming cultic in the enthusiasm of some of their followers. There is a danger, one hopes not for experienced counsellors, but often for novitiates and the public, that in the wish to promote counselling or to find comfort, an appeal to a deeply seated need might generate a new set of saviours. In doing this, or in responding to those needs with excessive claims to those who desperately search for a solution to end all solutions, the "triumph of the therapeutic", as Rieff titled it (1973), could in time find itself reduced to the status of those consumer durables that society has seized upon, exploited, found wanting, and discarded.

It is only by the most honest and realistic appraisal both of ideas about humankind, and of our therapeutic methods and beliefs, that we might avoid these errors ourselves. Any analysis, I suggest, cannot provide a solution, but the resources I highlight, and analysis of them, might act as a spur to wrestling with the issue. It is, of course, a huge question, with many suggestions through the ages regarding the problem of human nature, but it is a question that both the individual therapist or counsellor, as well as society at large, need to consider before throwing around epithets like "human nature is basically good" or "this person is evil".

Freud appears to have had no problem with the issue. He wrote to the Protestant minister, Pfister,

> I do not break my head very much about good and evil, but I have found little that is "good" about human beings on the whole. In my experience most of them are trash, no matter whether they publicly subscribe to this or that ethical doctrine or to none at all . . . If we are to talk of ethics, I subscribe to a high ideal from which most of the human beings I have come across depart most lamentably. [Meng & Freud, 1963, pp. 61–62]

It may come as something of a surprise to read such views from one who devoted most of his life to the investigation of the neurotic suffering of men and women, but such a personal statement confirms Freud's more public writing where he quite clearly views man as by nature narcissistic, non-altruistic, and pleasure-seeking. In a paper in 1908, for instance, he wrote, "Mastery through sublimation, diverting sexual energy away from its sexual goal to higher cultural aims succeeds with a minority . . . of the others most become neurotic or otherwise come to grief" (1908d, p. 88). Here he states the dilemma, as he saw it, of the relationship between the needs of the individual and the requirements of society in relation to sexuality. Equally pessimistic words can be quoted about the problem of aggression, this time from one of his followers: "[Man] is caught on the horns of a dilemma; either he must curb his aggressive instincts and suffer in the process himself, or he may give them free rein and cause suffering to others" (Wilbur & Muensterberger, 1951, pp. 148–149). As Guntrip comments about this, "Marie Bonaparte has given up as a bad job the possibility of the healthy socialisation of man" (1961, p. 70).

We could, of course, say that such descriptions are of the state of people as they are, and that it is the aim of therapy or analysis to change this situation and to rescue them from this dilemma. Clearly, their sexuality and aggression are two of the main problems that people find difficult to resolve without some cost to themselves or to others. But this would be a misleading aspiration, if we stay with Freud, because with him we are in the presence of a pessimistic outlook as well, not just a pessimistic analysis of the present situation. It is this that Jones, Freud's first biographer, records as Freud's self-description, although Jones himself disputes such a view (1964, p. 470). Freud was a perfectionist who found it difficult in some respects to tolerate deviation from the norm, particularly any deviation by his followers in the matter of the centrality of sexuality in aetiology, as well as deviation in his patients from certain codes of sexual behaviour. We must add that he was also a kind and caring man to many of his patients (see Chapter One, pp. 9–11), as well as to those colleagues whom he favoured.

To begin with he was more optimistic about the possibilities of success for analysis, and his followers often surpassed him in their enthusiasm. As Roazen comments: "Psychoanalysis began with the bold hope of freeing us from our mental conflicts. Its history, however, records a series of retreats in its claim for therapeutic efficacy" (1979, p. 32). Psychoanalysis was felt to be appropriate for all manner of ills (except perhaps psychosis), and in that first wave of success Freud wrote in 1913, "The time is not far distant when it will be generally recognised that no sort of nervous disturbance can be understood and treated without the line of approach and often the technique of psycho-analysis" (quoted by Roazen, 1979, p. 184). Others shared this idealization and optimism, like Binswanger, the Swiss psychiatrist, who wrote to Freud in 1911, "No success makes me proud, unless it is achieved by way of analysis", yet later reflected, "I still believed then that almost every patient must be analysed. It took ten years of hard work and disappointment before I realized that only a certain number of cases in our institution were suited to analysis" (*ibid.*, pp. 184–185). Freud's 1913 message is echoed twenty years later: "For me the time is not far distant when the more difficult field of the irreversible dynamic processes, which make up many chronic disorders of mankind, will be successfully invaded" (Jelliffe, 1933, p. 329).

Such optimism is not peculiar to analysis, and there have been many converts to other forms of therapy who have made such extravagant claims for their new-found methods. Nowhere is this more true than in that land of hope, the USA, a country which, in other matters, too, seems sometimes blind to its shortcomings. Again Roazen comments, "Psychoanalysis grew so fast as a movement that it has sometimes oversold itself as therapy; Americans in particular have been guilty of this" (1979, p. 186). For example, Janov, male midwife of primal therapy, makes the confident assertion: "If one theory is valid, and I believe Primal notions are valid, then other approaches are invalid", a remark that Kovel observes places him "in the ranks of the saviours who congregate in the history of therapy" (1978, p. 188).

However, Freud's optimism about the positive value of analysis was not to last, as one might expect with a man who developed his original ideas over a period of more than forty years. Even while Jelliffe was claiming future wonders, Freud had moved ground by 1933, so that he now commended analysis not as a method of treatment, but because of the truths it contains about human nature; as a method of treatment it is "one among many, though, to be sure, primus inter pares" (1933a, pp. 156–157)—slightly less extravagant than Jelliffe's or Janov's claim. Freud recognized limitations—he had already in 1908 said that a paranoid patient was not suitable for analysis. In a letter in 1932, he was "in general . . . skeptical about the effectiveness of analysis for the therapy of psychoses" (Deri & Brunswick, 1964, p. 106). Fortunately, others who have followed him and his method have shown how to adapt his therapy to the treatment of psychotic illness and shown that his pessimism in this direction was not warranted (e.g., Herbert Rosenfeld and Harold Searles, among others).

Freud's therapeutic hopes became more limited, though to be accurate we must acknowledge that he underlined that his approach was best for research, for knowledge about the mind, if not always for therapy itself. He foresaw that chemical methods would be able to correct psychological states, if the only concern was the cure of symptoms. He wrote to a pupil, "I should advise you to set aside your therapeutic ambitions and try to understand what is happening. When you have done that, therapeutics will take care of itself" (Roazen, 1979, p. 151). He even took the motto of an earlier surgeon, "I dressed his wounds, God cured him" (1912e, p. 115). In old age, Freud became more realistic and even more pessimistic, and we cannot exclude the possibility that this was also partially brought about by his own illness, the confirmation of life-long fears of death, and by the prevailing mood of post First World War Europe, when the optimism of the war-free years of 1871–1914 was shattered (a climate, incidentally, which affected other disciplines as well).

That post-war period saw the introduction of the death drive into Freud's thinking about aggression, but much of his early theory was influenced by the mechanistic scientific thinking of his time. He then saw what we might prefer to call emotional needs in terms of energy and drive, with increasing tension as the need to discharge those drives was blocked. That tension could not be relieved without the risk of exploiting others, because men and women live in a society with its explicit and implicit rules about sexual morality. Freud presents a bleak picture of the two alternatives to the expression of drives being, on the whole, adaptation to, or exploitation of, the needs of society. Civilization is based upon the suppression of the instincts. I have noted above how he thought that individuals differed in both the strength of their sexual instincts (1908d, p. 88) and in their capacity to re-channel those instincts into cultural aims, but his practical conclusion is that we have to sacrifice perfection in order to maintain what is possible, and so should relax the stringency of our sexual morality. Less sexual freedom would make people either rebel more openly, or suppress their desires and become more neurotic.

Thus, the Freudian view of humankind describes a situation not unlike that of the Pauline description of the inner warfare between the flesh and the spirit, between law and freedom (Romans, 7): a continual conflict between desire and morality, id and superego, between the needs of the individual and the good of the group. Freud appeared to suggest the need for the relaxation of sexual morality, although for himself, and quite clearly from reports we have of what he said to some of his patients, his own sexual ethic was strict. Between then and now, the gradual relaxation of sexual mores does not appear to have brought any diminution in the incidence of neurosis: indeed, many of the clients therapists see are still locked in by their personal issues, however much society has changed around them. That may suggest that sexual drives are, of course, no longer the major problem, but that personal relationships are. Furthermore, as drive theory gave way to object relations (which includes personal relations) theory, it is not just society, but the significance of early child–parent relationships that suggests equally great difficulties in later life.

Drive, or instinct, theory poses a conflict that is incapable of resolution without some degree of compromise and some suffering. It also portrays men and women as concerned only with the satisfaction or control of their own need for pleasure, with the consequence that others become the means of satisfaction, or agents of repression. Freud sees humankind as essentially narcissistic. That people can have positive regard for others, and can value close relationships that are based on more than sex, receives much less attention, at least in the earlier publications. Erich Fromm has suggested, however, that when Freud began to use the term "Eros" for the sexual instinct rather than "libido", he was beginning to see man not as primarily isolated and egotistical, but as related to others (1977, p. 590). It certainly is possible to detect such a change in him. In *Civilization and Its Discontents*, Freud could write, "What is the point of a precept enunciated with so much solemnity" (he was referring here to the commandment "Thou shalt love thy neighbour as thyself") "if its fulfilment cannot be recommended as reasonable" (1930a, p. 109). Yet, three years later, in his letter to Einstein "Why war?", he speaks of being able to have relations to others as loved objects, without having to have a sexual aim, and this time writes,

> There is no need for psychoanalysis to be ashamed to speak of love
> in this connection, for religion itself uses the same words, "Thou
> shalt love thy neighbour as thyself". This, however, is more easily
> said than done. [1933b, p. 264]

Fromm observes that Freud's view of human relations was partly
influenced by nineteenth century bourgeois ethics, based on the
principle of profit—what good will it do us to love another person?
Self-interest is still evident, and there is no pure altruism (Fromm,
1977, p. 592).

The death drive, or death instinct, referred to above appears at
first to be another of Freud's pessimistic ideas. It is, of course, controversial, even in psychoanalysis, so controversial that many of his
most ardent followers, with the notable exception of Melanie Klein,
have strongly qualified or rejected it. He turned his attention to the
problem of aggression after the First World War, seeing aggression
as the externalization of the death instinct. At the same time cancer
of his jaw was diagnosed, and he lost one of his daughters in the
Spanish flu epidemic. So was his gloomy picture of a drive towards
death an understandable but highly subjective idea? Freud thought
that fears are the conscious equivalents of unconscious wishes, so it
would not be surprising if he applied that axiom to the fear of
death, converting it into a wish for death. Yet in no sense did he
give in to death, continuing an energetic working life, despite the
debilitating effects of his cancer, to his death in 1939. His attitude to
life does not seem to bear out his theory.

But is that what his theory means? Perhaps it is not a gloomy
picture, but a realistic one: that we are moving towards death from
the moment of conception. What is for the most part kept in the
background, from time to time emerges as a more conscious recognition of this. These moments of recognition grow more frequent at
times of danger, or with increasing age. In addition, the death drive
has been interpreted in psychoanalysis as part of an ebb and flow
that continues throughout life, summarized by Maizels in this way:

1. There is a psychological tendency, in many ways corresponding
    to Freud's conception of the death instinct, towards achieving a
    permanent state of non-tension, non-effort, sleep, peace, passiv-
    ity and oblivion, and the phantasy or mental representation of
    this tendency is of reentering mother's womb.

2. With gradual physiological and ego development a new tendency "pushes" its way forwards. This tendency is characterized by desires for autonomy, independence and the overcoming of frustrations in the external world through effort.

3. These two tendencies are often felt to be in a state of conflict, particularly prior to the working through of the depressive position [that is the triumph of love over hate, of life over death, of the wish for dependence over autonomy or passivity over activity]. [Maizels, 1985, p. 188]

This is a less pessimistic, more realistic and recognizable interpretation of the death drive, and in any case Freud's drive theory in general has been eclipsed in analytical thought. Innate propensities there may be, but not in isolation from the environment. Sex may be felt by most people at some time as a driving force, particularly in adolescence, but, as Guntrip comments, those who have the most need to grasp at all sexual experiences presented to them, or who sexualize all relationships, are often those trying to compensate for the absence of love relationships when they were younger (1961, pp. 71, 76–77). Aggression similarly does not occur in isolation, rather when there is something to be angry about (even if this may be internally generated). Where relationships in childhood have been good, satisfying, and permanent, the ceaseless upsurge of powerful and demanding sexual impulses does not feature in experience except in realistic response to a truly appreciated external object. Guntrip says that it is not the struggle to live up to reasonable moral standards set by society that causes neurosis. Rather, it is neurosis which makes it difficult to live up to those standards (ibid., p. 77).

There is, of course, much more in Freud than this brief description. He also includes the effect of trauma, and implies that there is more hope in therapy where instinctual drive is less strong, and where trauma is the main cause of neurosis. Not that trauma should be understood in the sense that some people understand Freud from cursory knowledge, when they talk of a single event that has caused all the damage. There are, of course, catastrophic single events, but what is more common is a series of traumatic episodes—for example, a damaging relationship. In "Analysis terminable and interminable" (1937c) Freud writes about character, constitution and trauma. The stronger the constitutional factor (i.e., the strength of the instincts) the more a trauma leads to fixation. Analysis stands a better chance of being successful where the aetiology is traumatic rather than constitutional (1937c, p. 209ff). That essay is modest in its claims for analysis. Freud appears to view analysis as raising the power of resistance put up by inhibitions so that they can bear a heavier strain. Strengthen the defences, he seems to be saying, because you cannot free the drives themselves. Even so, he writes in that essay, only the optimist assumes that it is really possible to resolve a conflict between the ego and an instinct, finally, for all time. We cannot inoculate a patient against conflicts in the future.

The object-relations school is a development of Freudian theory. The difference between character and constitution on the one hand, and trauma in the sense of damaging early relationships on the other, is more pronounced, with the importance of early relationships regarded as more relevant than the strength of instincts, although there is still a place for innate characteristics—babies can, for example, be relatively passive or relatively active, without this being solely related to prenatal or immediate postnatal experiences.

Object relations is not just interested in external relationships, but also with internal objects—the internal figures built up from phantasized or actual experiences of external figures. Klein developed Freud's drive theory, and Kleinians put more emphasis on hate and aggression, as being part of a set of inner conflicts present in every child, although in some hate and aggression is innately stronger than in others. Kleinian thought is controversial even within a psychodynamic approach. Its relevance here is that there appears an element of fatalism about it. It implies that whatever external relationships are like, babies will experience hate and destructive rage against internal objects. Other analytic schools, such as the Middle Group, or Independents (e.g., Fairbairn, Winnicott) or the Freudians (following Anna Freud as well as her father) lay greater emphasis on the influence of external objects on the building up of inner objects and suggest that it is the trauma of being a baby with an imperfect set of parents that leads to difficulties in the inner world, which in turn influences the way the child copes with the external world. The greater the degree of deprivation, or inadequate mothering, the greater the difficulties in relationships later in life.

To be realistic, there is perhaps in practice not such a great difference between these various views: in practice no mother is perfect, all babies at some time or other are going to feel rejected and isolated, and even those whose mothers do not allow them to be deprived might err on the side of blurring those boundaries between mother and baby that are also essential to healthy development. All the analytic schools recognize that every baby has to learn to cope with rage and hate. But there is a difference, which is an important one, especially in theory, between positing, as Klein does, that destructive and suicidal ideas are the result of an innate death-instinct, and believing, as, for example, Winnicott does, that they are as a result of a failure of love and growth, and that it is within human power to make these failures good. There is a difference between what I perceive to be the Kleinian position, that love comes from a need to find security against, and to make reparation for, the anxiety of hate, and the Fairbairn–Winnicott view that sees love as a response to love in the early environment, a love that is capable of rendering hate less damaging.

Neither developmental model underestimates the difficulties that remain for the socialization of people. Guntrip, who is critical of Freudian theory, admits that the immediate task of society is still the same: to devise ways and means of coping with antisocial or neurotic behaviour, and to devise ways and means of improving social relations. But the basic theory, Guntrip feels, makes a difference to our views about the final possibilities of personal and social progress (1961, p. 80). Whatever the analytic school, the agreed position is that we are always struggling within our inner world, and that since the development of internal objects is inevitable, everyone has to deal with these conflicting inner relationships as well as with external relationships. That seems pessimistic, although it may ultimately be the most realistic position. But there is a difference between nature and nurture and between the view that, given a good enough upbringing, there is hope, against the Kleinian position that life is one long struggle between the paranoid–schizoid position and the depressive position. (Although the latter position is more positive, the very label given to it appears to suggest little joy!)

Whatever side of the balance one comes down on, psychoanalytic theory takes seriously the problems of love and hate. And whatever the developmental theory, none suggested abandoning hope, nor that theories about the importance of the early parental environment and/or innate characteristics excuse the abrogation of personal responsibility.

Taking love and hate seriously seems necessary for any therapy that tries to plumb the depths of human nature. There have been, however, critics of analysis, who have said that too much emphasis has been put on sexuality and aggression. One such critic was Ian Suttie, a psychiatrist who died just prior to the publication of his book, *The Origins of Love and Hate*, in 1963. He felt that the real taboo was not on sex, but on tenderness, and that the adult's incapacity for tenderness sprang from deficiencies in the first year of life. The cure of all ills seems to be the promotion of more love and more tenderness. Suttie says that even in the most passive therapy, the patient's need for love is met through the imperturbability and tolerance of the analyst, her or his patience, unfailing interest, ready memory, responsiveness, and insight. It is because patients feel loved that they can express anger, and then move through to a point where they feel unconditionally loved (1963, pp. 232–243).

Such a position, and indeed that put forward by Peter Lomas, for example, more recently (1973), has some similarity to the development in the USA of Carl Rogers's distinctive therapeutic theory and practice. The USA has been a very different milieu from Europe in terms of psychotherapeutic models and the whole human potential movement. The *angst* of European analysis, the doubts, ambiguity, and sometimes scepticism of Freudian analysis give way to key words like acceptance, nurture, tenderness, and joy. It scarcely needs spelling out, so pervasive has been his influence, that Rogers believes that no matter how seriously disturbed an individual, the only necessary and sufficient conditions for making constructive personality change are:

1. the client being in psychological contact with a therapist;
2. the client being vulnerable and anxious;
3. the therapist being integrated in the relationship.
4. the therapist having unconditional positive regard for the client;
5. the therapist being empathic and communicating this to the client. (1967, pp. 459–461).

As to therapeutic method, Rogers believes that the therapist should reinforce the positive esteem that a client should have for himself, and should create a positive climate by reflecting back what the client says in such a way as to reinforce that esteem. Treat a person in this way and the neurosis begins to break up and freedom is given to the true self to take over. This method has a counterpart in the psychoanalytic practice of supportive psychotherapy, where the approach likewise is to stress the positive features and achievements of the patient. As in all therapy, suggestion plays a part, and in this type of therapy and counselling it appears to play a significantly larger part.

Clearly, Rogers adopts a positive approach because theoretically he believes that human beings are basically good. He writes,

> One of the most revolutionary concepts to grow out of our clinical experience is the growing recognition that the innermost core of a man's nature, the deepest layers of his personality, the base of his "animal nature" is positive in nature—is basically socialised, forward moving, rational and realistic. [1974, pp. 70–71]

These seem to me to be assumptions that are more goals of therapy, or in life, than proven facts. One important question is whether every new baby is born with, as it were, a blank personality on which are inscribed the early and later learning experiences to make them what they become, or whether the baby is born with a script—a positive one in Rogers's view, or a rather more negative one in the view of Freudians and Kleinians should the initial experience be one of deprivation.

It would be misleading, however, to give the impression that Rogers is a pure optimist. Rogers writes in the same context,

> I do not have a Pollyanna view of human nature. I am quite aware that out of defensiveness and inner fear individuals can and do behave in ways which are incredibly cruel, horribly destructive, immature, regressive, anti-social, hurtful. Yet one of the most refreshing and invigorating parts of my experience is to work with such individuals and to discover the strongly positive directional tendencies which exist in them, as in all of us, at the deepest levels. [*ibid.*, p. 71]

As Kovel comments, the strength of the Rogerian approach is also its weakness (1978, p. 163). If a person is able to receive the message of unconditional positive regard, all well and good, but it is no simple task to accept that, with the result that self-loathing and inappropriate behaviours persist to different degrees in all of us, however supportive, loving, and warm others try to be. Recognition of negative feelings is essential. Here, the person-centred emphasis on empathy is more relevant than unconditional positive regard and love. As Rycroft writes in *Psychoanalysis Observed*, analysis can become a sort of replacement therapy with the effective agent in treatment being concern, devotion, and love. But why should the analyst consider that he possesses more love than his patient's parents? "Analysts who hold that their capacity to help patients derives from their ability to understand them . . . are really being more modest" (Rycroft, 1968, p. 17). Such understanding again seems more akin to Rogerian "empathy" than to "love".

This is not by any means to underestimate the importance of a warm and accepting attitude: Winnicott says, for instance, that "a belief in human nature and the developmental process exists in the analyst if work is to be done at all—and this is quickly sensed by the patient" (1958, p. 292). But the person who has not experienced tenderness in infancy needs something more than adult tenderness. However, it is simplistic to suggest that there is no more to person-centred practice than love and acceptance. Such qualities in the therapist provide the foundation for working with hate (as, for example, in Mearns and Thorne, 2000, pp. 58–59, a case vignette that recognizes the relationship of hate to an oppressive upbringing; nevertheless, the emphasis is still on the therapist's love).

Claiming to come somewhere between what Albert Ellis calls the polarity of Freudian pessimism and Rogerian optimism is rational emotive behaviour therapy (REBT, formerly RET), to which perhaps in this context could be linked other directive and active therapies, including behaviour modification. The rational–emotive therapist sees the two extreme views of humankind as mistaken. Humankind is not wholly biologically or historically determined, and always has the ability to reassess its imbibed values and to reindoctrinate itself. Such a view recognizes that we inherit strong instinctual tendencies, and go on behaving in a manner that even we can realize is self-defeating. So REBT acknowledges the irrationality of people, but says that human beings are unique in that they can understand their own limitations and can challenge themselves. Ellis believes that most disturbed people, such as psychopaths and psychotics, have a distinct biological or constitutional deficit, as well as being badly reared, and he sees them as intrinsically handicapped, never able to acquire the capacity to think straight. These people can be helped to live in some degree with their thinking--emotional handicaps, but can only be improved rather than cured.

But for the majority of suffering humankind he is more hopeful. Emotions are thought, not just felt, and he believes that blame is the essence of all human disturbance. The neurotic should stop blaming himself and others, and accept himself. REBT believes that people can make a definite change and conquer their basic hostility. The therapy sets out a dozen basic irrational beliefs, which individuals tend to hold, and which need to be challenged: e.g., the idea that as a human being you should be loved by every significant other person; or that one should be thoroughly competent, adequate and achieving; or that unhappiness is caused externally and that people cannot control themselves; or that the past is the all-important determinant of present behaviour (Ellis, 1967).

While Ellis seems to say that there is no virtue in optimism or pessimism, and that what therapy is trying to do is both rational and is based on reality, he is obviously being optimistic, at least as far as the possibilities of his therapy go for most people. When he writes "RET therapists believe that RET is not the *only* effective method of therapy, but simply that it is one of the *most effective* techniques that has so far been devised" (1967), he shows an optimism as strong as Rogers, whom Ellis accuses of being over-optimistic.

Is there a synthesis between the opposite poles of optimism and pessimism about the human condition and the possibilities for therapy? Ellis suggests one, the value of rationality, but with the recognition of some very damaged people making this impossible for them. More aligned with the analytic position is Jung, for whom the tension between opposites was an important part of his schema.

Jung takes evil seriously, like Freud. But he differs in a significant way, and makes a different yet valuable contribution to these issues. Freud's view of humankind as "trash" appears to suggest an attitude to the unconscious that sometimes seems to approximate to a rubbish tip, a waste dump, to which we consign all that we have not been able to cope with in our development; consequently, psychoanalysis seems sometimes to consist of grubbing around in the mess and the dirt, and re-encountering past conflicts so as to resolve them and then be able to leave them behind once and for all. It is perhaps inevitable that, as a pioneer, Freud's digging beneath the surface seemed like exposing a rubbish tip, and that he felt some discomfort in doing so. He is the one who has the muck on his hands and the taste in his mouth. But he invites others to view what he has found, and, having some of the dirty work done for them, they discover that it is not a rubbish tip, but almost like a prime archaeological find, with some precious treasures to be found in the dirt. The image is one that Freud used from his love of archaeology.

Jung's concept of the unconscious seems more positive: he delights in what he finds, and sees the unconscious as rich in treasure. And, thus, what Jung calls the archetype of the shadow he sees as an integral part of the personality, a part of us that we are to embrace and hold on to. The shadow is the complementary part, dark but not menacing. He writes,

> Since human nature is not compounded wholly of light, but also abounds in shadows, the insight in practical analysis is often somewhat painful, the more so if, as is generally the case, one has previously neglected the other side. [1935, par. 141).

Or, as he writes later in the same book,

> As the conscious mind can put the question, "Why is there this frightful conflict between good and evil?" so the unconscious can reply, "Look closer! Each needs the other. The best, just because it is the best, holds the seed of evil, and there is nothing so bad but good can come of it". [ibid., par. 183]

This is not to justify evil that good may come, but, in relation to therapy and the individual, does suggest that what is evil represents another side, perhaps a side that has been suppressed or has been forced to react against circumstances, and that by allowing that side to be expressed within the safety of the therapeutic relationship, there exist possibilities for change and positive development.

Jung comments on the nature of optimism and pessimism. He relates this to the process of analysis, and throws light on ways of viewing the modalities referred to in this chapter. Some patients, he says, begin to assimilate the unconscious, begin to feel more self-confident, and become full of themselves; they think they know everything about their unconscious, they think they understand themselves perfectly. But such optimistic self-confidence conceals a profound sense of impotence. In fact, such people are still fundamentally uncertain; and, commonly, therapists of this type develop a haughtiness, puffing up truths and needing to win followers to prove to themselves the value of their own convictions.

Then there is the reverse side of the coin, those people who feel themselves more and more crushed by the contents of their unconscious and lose their self-confidence. Jung believes that this pessimistic resignation masks a defiant need for power. Such people take their newly won insight to heart, forgetting that they are not unique in having a shadow side, getting unduly depressed, inclined to doubt everything, finding nothing right anywhere. Whereas the optimist has a desire to publish and proselytize, the pessimist may have some very good ideas, but can never bring her- or himself to make them public (Jung, 1935, par. 148). We cannot, perhaps, talk about optimism and pessimism in any particular theory and practice without recognizing that it is also a comment on the nature of the personality of the practitioners who write or talk about their position on the subject.

In Jung's description of two extremes we have examples of, on the one hand, attempts to master the shadow side too early, leading to inflation, and, in pessimism, a feeling of being overwhelmed by the shadow side. Jung suggests that the more people are able to assimilate the shadow part of themselves, the more they realize that they are like other people and that they are able to withdraw the projection of that shadow part on to other people which previously they have made. This in turn leads to identification with others, and love for others, since people come to realize just how much they have in common with others. However, all-out optimists, consciously, and all-out pessimists, unconsciously, want to be powerful people, leading others.

There are some similarities to this position in Erich Fromm's views on optimism and pessimism in his book *The Anatomy of*

Human Destructiveness. Fromm looks at the ambiguity of hope, and suggests that, outmoded though the term seems to have become in the contemporary western world, "faith" expresses an ardent and intense wish, which is different from optimism (1977, pp. 575–579). Optimism includes the quality of detachment, whereas faith implies personal concern. Rational faith, and its counterpart, which is rational despair, are based on thorough critical knowledge of all the factors involved.

In Fromm's opinion, optimism and pessimism in themselves seem to result in detachment and indifference. Fromm talks about this in relation to society. Optimists believe in the march of progress, and so are alienated from the threats that the future might hold. Pessimists are, in practice, scarcely any different, because their pessimism acts similarly as a protection against the inner demand to do something by saying that nothing can be done: the optimist protects himself by saying that nothing needs to be done. But "to have faith means to dare, to think the unthinkable, yet to act within the limits of what is realistically possible" (*ibid.*, p. 579).

Fromm, in common with other neo-Freudians, attaches more significance to the wider environment, the society in which the individual is brought up and lives, often missing in those schools that concentrate intensely upon the individual and appear to attribute little significance to culture, sub-culture, and the socio-economic factors that contribute so importantly to individual fortunes. It is necessary, then, to recognize the important questions that the more radical therapies ask: how change can take place in individuals without changing the society in which they live, and the pressures to which they are therefore subject. Individual therapy, in this view, is just tinkering with the edges.

Faced with despair on a European scale during and following the Great War, Freud turned to the problem of aggression and developed the concept of the death drive. Jung represented a very different view to that of the later radical therapies that changes within individuals would change societies. In 1918 he wrote,

> The spectacle of this catastrophe threw man back upon himself by making him feel his complete impotence; it turned his gaze inwards, and, with everything rocking about him, he must needs seek something that guarantees him a hold. Too many still look

outwards, some believing in the illusion of victory and of victori-
ous power, others in treaties and laws, and others again in the overthrow of the existing order. But still too few look inwards, to their
own selves, and still fewer ask themselves whether the ends of
human society might not be best served if each man tried to abol-
ish the old order in himself, and to practise in his own person and
in his inward state those precepts, those victories which he
preaches at every street corner, instead of always expecting those
things of his fellow men. Every individual needs revolution, inner
division, overthrow of the existing order, and renewal, but not by
forcing them upon his neighbours under the hypocritical cloak of
Christian love, or the sense of social responsibility, or any of the
other beautiful euphemisms for unconscious urges to personal
power. Individual self reflection, return of the individual to the
ground of human nature, to his own deepest being with its individual and social destiny—here is the beginning of a cure for the
blindness which reigns at the present hour. [1918, p. 5]

Having reviewed the implicit or explicit optimism and
pessimism in a number of representative modalities, what does this
say about the therapeutic task? Other therapists will surely have
shared my experience that there have been clients about whom I
have been optimistic and yet ultimately disappointed about what
therapy has achieved for them, and other occasions when I have felt
extremely pessimistic and consequently surprised by the changes
that have taken place during therapy. This suggests trying not to
make judgements or predict results. Better, where possible, to adopt
a neutral stance about what the past suggests or the future holds.
In any event, the "success" of therapy is not to be measured in those
terms. This is perhaps an attitude that is shared by psychodynamic
and person-centred practitioners, in both modalities concerned
more for the centrality of the therapeutic relationship than with
actively seeking change. Change, where it happens, follows from
that relationship, and its fostering of different facets in the client. (It
is what is fostered that gives rise to less agreement between the two
modalities.)

Many of the therapies that have evolved from, or in antithesis
to, the analytic have helped to broaden the analytic perspective.
They have focused attention upon the emotions and have balanced
the intense concentration on the mind and the unconscious that was

Freud's legacy. They have, on the whole, been optimistic about the possibilities for change. Neo-Freudian therapies have introduced another dimension, the political context, society, culture, and the wider world. Some therapies have concentrated upon symptom change. And that, of course, is what many clients—and funders—seek.

For myself, as a therapist I do not neglect the goals that bring people to therapy, but I do not seek to concentrate upon them. I cannot but see therapy as providing the setting for a process of slow change, yet I share this with the behaviourists: that where there is change, it is more as a result of modification than of radical revolutionary change. I am more of an evolutionist than a revolutionary. People learn how to avoid some of the conflicts that previously have troubled them; they learn, perhaps, to be more assertive, but still have to work at being so; they sometimes remain depressed, or subject to depression, but become more able to tolerate it and work through each episode. They learn about self-reflection. It seems to me that to be a revolutionary in outlook a person needs to be optimistic and somewhat arrogant, to feel that they know what solutions will work. As an evolutionist I know that there are some changes, in both the individual and in society, which will become blind alleys and reach dead-ends. But I do not know which will be so, and so can never know, in advance, whether any particular change is right or not. Revolutionaries are very single-minded, whereas evolutionists believe much more in diversification, knowing that some changes will survive, while others may contain the seeds of their own destruction. Both revolutionaries and evolutionists examine the past and speak of the present, but the evolutionist does not attempt to predict the future. So, as a therapist, I may be able to help people to look at their past and at their present situation, but I cannot know what for them is the right future. It is my impression of some therapies that they set up standards of what people should be like, and have norms for what makes a rounded human being.

There is another aspect of an evolutionary stance. It is that change takes place not only within each individual, but also from generation to generation. Erikson makes the point graphically in the phrase: "Healthy children will not fear life if their elders have integrity enough not to fear death" (1964, p. 261). It is by a process of what often is slow and painstaking work with today's parents, and today's future parents, to help them change a little, one hopes, but, equally important, to help them achieve sufficient insight to be able to bring up their children in the light of their own therapeutic experience. I do not mean the type of reaction against their own childhood that could become equally imposing on their own children, such as, "I was so disciplined as a child, my children will be able to do as they like"; or, "My parents made me do such and such and I shall ensure my children do the same". There is another way, which, I used to find as a university counsellor, seemed to be hinted at by some of the young adults I worked with: "I'm looking forward to having children; I would like them to grow up to understand some of the things I am only just beginning to understand now". Of course, those future parents would make mistakes too, and would not always be able to be so high-minded, and even their good intentions might have resulted in some mistakes. That does not invalidate the hope for positive development that therapists have for their clients: that it is not just about change in terms of the present, but about links backwards and forwards on a time scale that is so much greater than a single life span.

Like those young adults with whom once I worked, I have hope, tempered, as long as I can keep unreliable optimism or pessimism at bay, by the reality of knowing that outcomes are unpredictable. Helping people find a similar attitude might be the one obvious objective of therapy.

CHAPTER FIVE

The therapist's revenge: the law of talion as a motive for caring

I t is almost customary for therapists who write to thank their patients or clients—and rightly so, since the most stimulating learning (which with adaptation is often transferable to other client work) comes from insights or ideas that emerge in the material that clients bring to therapy. This paper was one such, solely brought to life by the case example of Brenda (not, of course, the client's name, although the details are factual). Brenda provided another example that I was able to use in teaching and in a different book, although one that taught me to take greater care in disguising client material so that even the client herself could not recognize it. I will say no more, except to say I was very grateful to a co-therapist who handled that situation so well that Brenda and I emerged on good terms. It was my mistake, but I wonder whether there was a type of revenge in the incident. On my part, of course, for being in debt to her for the idea she planted and that bore fruit in what at the time seemed (and perhaps is) original.

* * *

I need to start with a health warning, because a colleague to whom I sketched out the ideas I present here responded with a vigorous protest at what I was proposing, and threatened to write a paper in reply. I hesitate to say that I had touched a soft spot, and that this gave me some confidence that my theme was therefore a justifiable one to propose to therapists. If I do so I may simply be getting revenge at some distance for my colleague's protest. But it may be desirable, given the provocation implicit in the title of this chapter, to preface it with the reminder that I am not writing about what is right or wrong, or about whether revenge in the therapist is or is not a "good thing". My objective is to take one rather neglected feature of human relatedness that might be examined in relation to the helping relationship as much as it can be studied in the context of other relationships.

Human emotions from time to time need to be reinstated as being natural, and perhaps even in beneficial, and not simply pathological. What Freud did for sexuality and Klein for aggression means that today, at least as therapists, we think nothing of saying that sexuality and aggression are part and parcel of the human condition; that they have at the very least to be acknowledged and, when aroused, appropriately expressed and worked through; and that they are present in different strengths in the therapeutic relationship, in client and therapist. Susan Jacoby, the author of a book on revenge, notes that it is a taboo subject in our society (1983). She draws upon a paper by Kohut (1971) in which he recognizes aggression and revenge as legitimate forces in the personality, towards which we need to overcome our hypocritical attitude. Jacoby writes,

> It will not do to classify vengeance as merely childish, because it is decidedly adult . . . Like sex before Freud, revenge is condemned as immature and undesirable and thus unworthy of serious scientific investigation. This hypocrisy neither does justice to our profession nor does it contribute to a better understanding of destructive human aggression. [1983, p. 169]

Neither does such hypocrisy contribute to a better understanding of the creative aspects of revenge. Like envy and jealousy, this is another deep emotion that is not necessarily bad. Revenge within the therapist may act as one of the legitimate motives for caring.

Perhaps the ambivalence towards the concept of revenge can be put another way by contrasting the Old and the New Testament attitudes to the law of talion or the law of retaliation: the law of doing to others what has been done to you. The Old Testament commended the principle of "an eye for an eye, a tooth for a tooth" (Exodus 21: 24). The Sermon on the Mount apparently commended the antithesis of this in "turn the other cheek" (Matthew 5: 9); but it also introduced a variation on the law of talion, reversing the direction from a reactive response to a proactive position: "Judge and you will be judged . . . forgive and you will be forgiven . . . treat others as you would like them to treat you" (Matthew 7: 1, 12).

Therapists in particular, through their own therapy, should not have naïve views about the nature of the caring relationship. What is offered in therapy is much more than the attempt to do good, to be kind and to wish clients well. Therapists, in the course of their training, come to recognize that they are not motivated solely by goodness, kindness, and well-wishing. They learn to acknowledge that as therapists they act with what at times looks suspiciously like sadistic, seductive, or salacious interest towards their clients, albeit in what they hope is controlled and sublimated form. The value of this deeper understanding of ourselves is that in accepting these aspects of their humanity, and avoiding their excesses, they can allow them to be integrated positively within the therapeutic process.

In examining the theme of revenge, it should not be confused with another of the wishes that is believed to be one of the motivations for being a therapist: the need to make reparation. The difference between the two might be expressed as this: reparation is one possible response to the damage we did or imagine we did to others; revenge is one possible response to the damage we had, or felt we had, done to us. In our past we have learnt what it means to hurt and also to be hurt, and, in becoming therapists, we wish to put right (via displacement on to others) some of the damage we have seen, have experienced, or have even caused others in the past. I suggest that it is not only reparation that is displaced or sublimated, but also revenge.

This difference between making reparation, and feeling and, indeed, expressing revenge, is illustrated in a client's story that provided the starting point for my thinking about this whole theme. It is a story where it seems that revenge made the helper feel better, without damaging anyone else. Such a positive view of revenge is perhaps reflected in the words often associated with the feeling. We speak of a "thirst" or a "yearning" for revenge and of the fulfilment of that wish as "sweet revenge" (Durham, 1990). Such phrases indicate a sense of satisfaction and fulfilment.

Brenda, as the client might be called, was a young woman who originally went for counselling because she was unable to grieve the death of her father. The link between revenge and unresolved grief is identified as essential by Searles (1956), and I return to the relationship between these two emotions below. Brenda understandably found it hard to mourn her father, because the latter had died in Southern Africa, after emigrating there when Brenda was eight or nine. Her father had separated from her mother long before that, and Brenda's memories of him were few, nearly always associated with standing as a little girl by her mother's side, trying to act as a buffer between her mother and father on his occasional visits. Brenda therefore had no relationship to mourn: she was more likely to need to mourn the absence of a relationship with her father.

Brenda's mother entered a new and permanent relationship when Brenda was about ten. Her stepfather was not an easy man to live with, and as Brenda grew older she was perpetually irritated by the stepfather's ignorant and crass attitudes. She not unnaturally resented the intrusion of this man into the household, and this was also seen in the transference relationship, where her anxiety at having to share was seen as being connected with sharing her mother with another person. Incidentally, since I allude to child abuse below, Brenda had been sexually abused by a woman lodger when she was five, and Brenda attempted to seduce her new and younger stepsister when Brenda was fifteen. That felt like a type of revenge, both upon her seductress and upon her stepfather: she may not have been able to get at either, but she could get at a substitute. The ability to take revenge out on others, in place of the one upon whom revenge was or is most appropriately sought, is a feature we need to bear in mind throughout. Freud alludes to an article by Rank in which he gave examples of acts of revenge carried out against the wrong people, retelling a rather sick joke which he calls "the comic story of three village tailors, one of whom had to be hanged because the only village blacksmith had committed a capital offence" (1923b, pp. 385–386).

Brenda had her chance of revenge, but also an opportunity to express grief, which she did not avoid. About six months into therapy her stepfather fell terminally ill and was given only a few months to live. The implications of this were thought through (it was not yet possible to feel them through), including what it might be like for Brenda when her stepfather died. Therapy temporarily ceased before that happened, and Brenda left the district for a few months, spending much of her time at her mother's home. She was there from the time when her stepfather returned from hospital to the day after the funeral. She then returned to make contact with her therapist and told her story of what seemed to her therapist to be an example of caring revenge.

In the final weeks that she had spent in her mother's home, Brenda gave a large of amount of herself in supporting her mother and in helping to nurse her stepfather. At times she spoke out for her stepfather, especially when she thought her mother or the visiting nurse were misunderstanding the dying man, and treating him somewhat as an unfeeling object. She eased the man's dying as much as she could, and stayed with him through his final hours, ensuring he was as comfortable as possible to the last. After her stepfather's death she helped to lay out the body, and she recounted in detail a rather gruesomely amusing story about the man's jaw continuously dropping. Although she did not realize this can happen to a corpse, the detail may be relevant.

Brenda was clearly deeply moved by having been through this experience. There was an obvious sense in which she had made some sort of reparation for the hostile feelings she had nursed through her adolescence right up to this last year of her stepfather's life. Formulated in another way, we might say that she was involved in an undoing of the strained and distant relationship of the past: if we are cynical, as psychoanalytic formulations sometimes appear, we might even say she was reacting against her death wishes towards the man, and doing what she could to make the quality of the final weeks of his life richer. Another of Brenda's presenting problems had been feeling and expressing hostility. Brenda was certainly proud, and justifiably so, that she had not flinched from spending so much time with a dying man or from handling the dead body with the jaw that kept opening.

But there was more to this series of events than all that. Brenda described, with considerable insight into her present state of mind, what she was doing, now that she had returned to her friends. She was telling them about the things that had happened, and she recognized that one reason for talking to them was to try to work through the grief and pain that she had experienced. But there was more to her speaking about it than that. She added, "I reckon that what I'm doing in telling them about all the details of the last few weeks is letting them know that I'm better than he [the stepfather] was to me, that at least I could treat him well, even though he didn't treat me well." What was clear as Brenda said this was that her tone was not one of making reparation; the expression in her voice was one of exacting a kind of revenge upon the dead man. Although Brenda recognized that she was doing this as she told her story to her friends, perhaps she was also doing this to the dying man while he was alive, because in all her acts of caring for the stepfather she was saying to him, "You didn't ever do this for me, but I'm doing it for you". Is that why, in Brenda's eyes, his jaw continued to drop, speechless yet amazed?

This type of revenge, which Durham calls "constructive vengeance" (1990), is also seen in one of her case vignettes. It is another illustration of a type of revenge that comes from doing better than the one who has hurt you, although there was more obvious self-interest in its consequences than Brenda's constructive vengeance showed. Mr B was a polished jazz musician, in manner somewhat mild and even apologetic. He was depressed because he had been deeply hurt by his lover, herself a musician in his group. He looked at his anger in therapy, and his energy slowly returned as he began to practise his saxophone with new vigour. One day he announced in therapy that he had vowed to outshine his lover in his performance. "Living well is the best revenge," he said at one point, although later in the session he reflected that he could have a lot more fun by being furious.

Doing well, caring well, living well—is there an element of revenge in the therapist outshining those who have hurt him or her in the past? If we begin to admit the possibility of revenge as one of the motives for being a therapist, there is confirmatory evidence in at least one illustrious predecessor. Freud tells a story in *The Interpretation of Dreams* (1900a, p. 197) that his father had in turn told him, of his father as a young man, walking in the streets of a town where Freud was born, when a Christian knocked off his cap, yelling at Freud's father, "Jew, get off the pavement." Freud had asked his father how he had responded, and his father had replied that he did nothing, but went into the road to pick up his cap. Freud recalled that he contrasted this situation, of his father telling him this story of unheroic conduct, with that of the ancient Carthaginian general Hannibal: Hannibal's father had made his son swear vengeance on the Romans for what the Romans had done to him. Freud writes that "ever since that time Hannibal had had a place in my phantasies". One of Freud's biographers, Peter Gay, draws partly upon this incident when he suggests that two of the motives for Freud's life's work were "the need for revenge and self-vindication" (1989, p. 23). This looks like another example of "constructive vengeance", of the way in which the wish for revenge is turned into a powerful force that is potentially for good.

There is possibly another example of the same phenomenon in the effects of sexual abuse. I referred earlier to Brenda's experience of sexual abuse as a child, and as an adolescent trying to seduce her younger stepsister as a type of revenge. There is evidence to suggest that some of those who are abused as children either become abusers themselves ("an eye for an eye") or that some enter one of the caring professions, where they are likely to be involved in part in helping others who have been abused. There may be no connecting strand between these alternative outcomes, but it is worth speculating whether the same law of talion lies beneath either direction that an abused person may take, in the one case leading to destructive revenge, the other to constructive vengeance: "it may have been done to me, but I will not do it to you". Indeed, the thinness of the line between repeating abuse and healing or preventing abuse may account for the way in which a few people tragically slip from caring into abusing those who have entrusted to them. Like Oedipus, they cannot in the end resist the force of the Fates.

It is dangerous, of course, to take a few examples and to extrapolate from these to say that all therapists and counsellors are motivated, at least partially, by the wish for revenge, even if I make it more palatable by calling it "constructive vengeance". Yet to do so, if for the moment only for the sake of argument, has at least the merit of alerting us to potentialities within the therapeutic relationship for the destructive or the constructive use of the thera-pist's revenge. It is these to which I now turn.

Revenge is seen in its constructive mode in Brenda's case: revenge provides an incentive to care better than she had been cared for by her stepfather. It is similar to that wish which many growing children have, that they should not repeat the mistakes they perceived that their parents made with them. In due course, it turns out that some of these perceived mistakes are unavoidable, and that from a parent's point of view, if not from the child's, they are sometimes not mistakes at all. But there is always the hope that the succeeding generation will do things a little better than the generation before, and that their doing so will make it easier for the next generation to do even better than them. That hope needs to be tempered with the recognition that we do not necessarily do much better, that sometimes we make different mistakes and that on occa-sions we may even do worse. Constructive revenge needs to be seasoned with the wisdom to know that what starts out as an attempt to be different can end up being the same. (The "return of the repressed"?) The unconscious wish for "an eye for an eye" does not disappear merely by wishing it so. The Fates have a way of catching us out (see Chapter Nine).

A second way in which revenge is potentially constructive is when hate or anger, a vital part of revenge, is channelled towards just ends. The notion of a just cause is a difficult one, and tends, of course, to be open to a subjective interpretation of what is just. What is just to the avenger may seem like hypocrisy to another. Nevertheless, "righteous wrath" is one of four positive aspects of revenge summarized in an essay by Searles (1956) from an article titled "The value of vindictiveness", written by Karen Horney (1948). The concept of righteous wrath also appears in Durham's article on revenge, illustrated by the need for Israel to take revenge on those who carried out the policy of extermination of so many Jews. Righteous wrath also involves keeping alive the memory of the injustice. She quotes Eli Wiesel: "Come and learn what human beings do to other human beings. Learn the limits of humanity. Learn, and hope is possible. Forget, and despair is inevitable" (Durham, 1990). Although keeping alive a *memory* may be a constructive way of gaining revenge ("I'll not let you forget this"), in a private conversation I remember well one Jewish woman who had suffered telling me that for her the ultimate revenge for the camps was to be able to survive and to survive well. Some abuse victims, on the other hand, also determined to survive, survive and yet perhaps hope that their suffering will then perpetuate the abuser's guilt, at least in their phantasy. The problem is, should they then in fact only inflict damage upon themselves?

Atrocities such as the holocaust or abuse raise the question of justice, and it is worth remembering that the allegorical figure of justice is a blindfolded woman holding in one hand a pair of scales. Justice, while it metes out punishment, also requires balance, so that, as in the law of talion, there can be restoration of balance. Achieving the correct balance is what makes talion so difficult to achieve, so that it is not endlessly perpetuated, with the weight on each side getting heavier and heavier each time. In an unpublished paper, a counsellor working in a law school thinks that the choice of the legal profession sometimes appears to hinge upon the idea of justice as a symbol of moral retribution. As she puts it, describing her students, "There is a consistent idealization of justice—a cling-ing to the notion that the law protects the victim, that justice will administer punishment to the perpetrator on behalf of the victim" (Farrell, 1994). She cites examples of lawyers in training, who were her clients, whose family circumstances, like Brenda's, can make us understand their need for revenge.

I have already linked the massive abuse and consequent revenge experienced by or on behalf of those killed or maimed in the camps, with individual victims (particularly children) of sexual, physical, and psychological abuse. Unfortunately, in many such cases, there is no system of justice that properly meets the desire for revenge, either because the law is powerless to act or convict, or because even when it does the sentence does not appear to the victim to make amends. Nevertheless, it is interesting to find that perhaps another profession has as one of its motives the need to deal with the need for revenge. Through the work they do, lawyers perhaps displace their need for vengeance either on their own behalf or on behalf of their clients. But how does a therapist deal with the passionate anger she may feel in herself or on a client's behalf? A colleague recounts how angry and vengeful she felt towards the man who had abused her client when she was a child. Although the therapist longed to express revenge by telling her client just what she felt (and, had it been possible, the male abuser, too), her sense of righteous wrath was directed towards strengthening the woman's ability to get rid of this still menacing figure, partly internalized, but partly still around in her life. The therapist, waiting her moment, said to her client, "It somehow doesn't seem right that this man took away all your childhood; and now there is a danger of him spoiling your whole adult life too. It feels like he needs to be given a very strong message to go away and leave you alone, which is just what you couldn't do when you were a little girl."

A second example in similar vein is of a client who was encouraged in her distress to imagine what she would like to do to the man who abused her. She phantasized pushing her abuser out of the front door, down the garden path, and under a big red double-decker bus. Then the client became worried about her therapist's reaction to this phantasy involving such violent thoughts of revenge. However, far from being shocked or censorious, the therapist was able to support the client's imaginative ability to exact revenge as illustrating her need to get the man out of her inner world, so that she could be free of his threats.

There is a problem should the therapist meet a client who is actually planning revenge, and who might carry it out. However appropriate righteous wrath is, given some of the appalling circumstances calling for revenge, acting it out is inappropriate. Revenge can give another spin to the cycle of violence.

An example that illustrates the value of the phantasy of revenge on the one hand, and yet the danger of acting it out on the other, is described at length in Masud Khan's book *Our Hidden Selves* (1983, pp. 139–180). Khan takes the reader step by step through a difficult and tantalizing therapeutic relationship with a man who saw himself as hopelessly evil. As the man's story unfolded, Khan learnt that his patient, as a young man of fourteen, had been knocked off his bicycle by an overtaking car. His right arm and hand were crushed and were almost useless. But Khan's patient developed a sexual phantasy, which Khan saw as a type of playful revenge upon the car, but one that changed the man's prospects from despair and hopelessness to overcoming his disability. The phantasy came about as the result of an episode that must have reminded his patient to some extent of the accident: in this episode two girls cycled past him;

the sight of them sexually excited him, and triggered off in him an elaborate phantasy that involved hitting the girls, just as the car had once hit him. The man translated this phantasy at first into drawings, but then was able to displace the sexual stimulus into learning and perfecting the craft of furniture making. In the drawing and the exercise of his craftsmanship he was able to recover much of the use of his arm and hand, as well as his self-respect. Khan comments on the way the vengefulness, expressed initially in the playful sexual phantasy, ultimately was turned towards a very positive purpose. Unfortunately, a later, one-off sexual episode turned the man's phantasy into reality, in which he acted out his sadistic feelings, and it is clear that this acting out of revenge threatened to destroy the man's whole life's work, as well as his sense of pride and hope.

This case confirms other points in Horney's article (1948), where she suggests that revenge, or vindictiveness, as she calls it, serves a positive function. Vindictiveness helps to restore injured pride; it provides the hope of triumph and the prospect of success; and it helps to repress hopelessness. In Khan's example, the inappropriate acting out of the man's revenge in a sadistic sexual act crushed his achievements in all three ways, just as the overtaking car had originally crushed his arm and hand. Acting out revenge risks turning constructive revenge into revenge that is equally destructive of the avenger.

There are other dangers in certain aspects of revenge within the therapeutic relationship that must be set against the value that I have so far assigned to the concept. There are, first, all manner of ways, some small and some large, in which therapists and clients take out their revenge on one another. The phrase "tit for tat" often refers to some of the smaller examples of the law of talion: when, for example, a client misses a session following one where the therapist has let the client down; or where the therapist starts the session late following a client being late for the therapist. They are not always insignificant events in the course of therapy, but they need not take up much space in this context.

There are larger, more subtle examples of the therapist's revenge that merit greater attention. Racker, in his book on transference and countertransference (1968), uses the phrase "the vengefulness of silence" as an example of the effects of negative countertransference on the part of the therapist who feels badly treated by the client.

Similarly Searles refers to the retaliatory demands which therapist and patient can make upon each other: the patient demands relief from suffering, the therapist demands greater self-awareness than the patient yet possesses (Searles, 1962, p. 589). Searles' use of the term "retaliatory" is an indication of the vengeful quality of these mutual demands, which he sees as a defence against the growing fond contentment that therapist and patient have in each other. In the same essay, Searles looks at another side of this fond contentment, whereby what he calls a "prolonged stalemate" develops between therapist and patient, in which the therapist seems determined to keep the patient ill and so avert the loss of the close relationship between them (*ibid.*, p. 591). Although Searles does not use the term retaliation in this particular context, he seems to suggest that there is an aspect of revenge in this determination to keep the patient ill, since his earlier paper on the psychodynamic of vengefulness clearly links revenge with both grief and separation-anxiety. It is possible to draw two conclusions from Searles about the possibilities for the expression of revenge on both sides of the therapeutic relationship: that the patient may experience the need for revenge towards the therapist for not making him or her better quickly enough, and that the therapist may feel vengeful towards the patient for getting better too quickly.

If these are subtle examples of the possibilities for revenge within the therapeutic relationship, which in differing degrees may prove to have a destructive component to them, my final example may be even less obvious. Having contrasted destructive revenge with constructive revenge, there is an interesting contrast between the need for revenge and forgiveness. Forgiving a person who has hurt you does not magically remove the wish for revenge. Yet the person who has been forgiven does not expect any further retaliation, and in an ideal world the act of forgiveness also means some relief for the person who does the forgiving.

Forgiveness is not as straightforward as might be assumed. "I won't apologize, but let's forgive and forget," said an old Coventry fire-fighter, as he reflected back upon the blanket bombing of Dresden. His moral struggle is evident: he wants to find a way to be reconciled with former enemies, but he still feels the superiority of his own position. He might even have wanted the other party to do the forgiving and forgetting, without by any apology having to give way himself. His words provide an example of the delicate balance there is in all relationships: he does not feel happy at the other side being left in an inferior position, but neither does he want to risk being put down himself. No wonder revenge and retaliation is such a common feature in human relating, because it is an attempt to restore a fragile balance. If revenge is often unsuccessful it is because the balance goes too far the other way, demanding its own retaliation. Did Dresden balance out Coventry? Or did it put the Allies in the dock?

Yet it is not simply that it is difficult to forgive. It is also difficult to be forgiven, and there may be an element of revenge in forgiving experienced by the person who is forgiven. Forgiveness and retaliation are more than two sides of a coin: they are not as opposite as they first appear. Like the two faces of the same coin, they are linked. Although Brenda's care of her dying stepfather illustrates constructive revenge, there is a negative dimension of forgiveness. For instance, how might Brenda's stepfather have felt had he realized some of Brenda's motivation for caring for him? Similarly, therapists might ask what the effect on their clients might be of their care of them, their acceptance of them, their not judging them, and even their implicit forgiveness of them in therapy through this non-judgemental attitude? There is a danger, which should not be overstated, but is nevertheless worth considering, that what therapists see as positive attitudes and as the opposite of vengefulness, might be experienced at least by some clients as an expression of our unconscious punitive revenge.

The same law of talion suggests that there may be a subtle link between forgiveness and revenge. "Forgive and you will be forgiven" may be closer to "an eye for an eye" than is immediately apparent. This possibility arises from a particular reading of one of the parables that Jesus told, a story which has at its heart problems associated with forgiveness. It is possible, of course, to use such stories without having to associate them with the whole panoply of Christian theology in which they have become embedded.

The story is apparently told in response to the question "How many times should I forgive my brother?" Jesus tells of a king who decided to settle all his accounts. One of the first of those to appear before him was a man whose debt ran into many millions, but he had no means of paying. His master ordered him and his family and his possessions to be sold; but he was so moved when the man pleaded for more time to pay that he forgave him the whole debt. The man who had been forgiven left the king, and immediately ran into a fellow servant who owed him a few pounds; he caught him by the throat, and demanded his money back. Despite the pleas that he give his fellow servant more time to pay, he threw him into jail. In turn, the story concludes, his master commanded the unforgiving servant to pay his debt in full (Matthew 18: 23–34).

Stories such as this can be understood in many different ways, but that is part of their fascination. It is a slender plot, but it bears this interpretation: that one of the reasons why the servant who had the large debt remitted was unable to forgive his fellow servant was because he did not himself feel forgiven. On the surface he had obviously been let off his debt; his master was generous and apparently forgave him everything. Yet, in doing so, the master had, in a moral sense rather than a financial one, forgiven one debt only to create a different one. He put his servant even more greatly in his debt by wiping the financial state clean. In the power balance this servant was doubly obliged to his master, indebted for being let off the financial debt.

The servant's reaction accords with the law of talion, which could have gone either way. He could have forgiven the fellow servant his debt, as he himself had been forgiven, and in so doing he could have experienced some relief from his own feelings of indebtedness. As it was, the law of talion went the other way, fastened perhaps more on the feeling of powerlessness towards the forgiving king. It was translated into restoring the power balance, through displacing it on to another relationship in which the servant could experience the destructive, rather than the constructive, power of revenge. Forgiveness, acceptance, and generosity of care can be a very powerful means of exerting a hold or pressure over another person, especially if we do not let the other forget what we have done for them, nor how selfless we have apparently been. Forgiveness can be a type of revenge. Retaliating with an eye for an eye at least creates equality, if not always equilibrium.

There is certainly much support in the behaviour of the pre-Reformation church for casting a suspicious eye on forgiveness, especially where the retaliatory element has been repressed but appears in another form. Penance and forgiveness became an industry, a huge balance sheet in which days in purgatory meant as much to the ordinary believer then as credit card accounts mean today: "How much do I owe? What have I got to pay off?" The forgiveness business became a way of exerting power over people, particularly over the lower orders of society, although excommunication (the ultimate sign of non-forgiveness) became a political weapon that could be used against princes.

The therapeutic relationship also provides possibilities for forgiveness and revenge. Therapy is sometimes seen as the modern confessional, and the therapist as the contemporary priest. If this is at all the case, then the equivalent of the revenge in forgiveness may even be what we call "the therapeutic attitude". Therapists may not pronounce forgiveness, but they try to provide an accepting, non-judgemental milieu in which the client may come to some sense of reconciliation with the past, with memories, with parts of the self, and with other people. The milieu is powerful, and, indeed, the power of the therapist's position has certainly been recognized by many before me (e.g., Guggenbuhl-Craig, 1971). "Remember how I forgave you" does not always have to be put into words to put the forgiven at a disadvantage. "Look what I have given you" similarly does not have to be spoken to put the client in the therapist's debt. The generosity involved in each of these ways of relating can put the recipient at into a humbled position, but also sometimes into a humiliated position. Therapists may claim that the client's fee (their gift to the therapist) restores the balance, and enhances the client's self-respect. I doubt whether it is equal to the debt that a grateful client owes to a good therapist.

Can we ever pay back? Can we ever forgive? Eli Wiesel seems to have been less ambivalent than the Coventry fire-fighter when he prayed at Auschwitz, "God of forgiveness, do not forgive those who created this."

There is a different outcome in Shakespeare's comedy *As You Like It*, where Orlando, who has been maltreated by his elder brother Oliver, chances upon Oliver asleep in the forest, about to be attacked by a lioness. Oliver himself describes how Orlando twice turned his back on his brother,

> But kindness, nobler than revenge,
> And nature, stronger than his just occasion,
> Made him give battle to the lioness . . . [5. 2. 129–131]

In this case revenge was so easy—just by walking away Orlando could have exacted it; but if kindness is described as nobler than revenge, the phrase "killing with kindness" should be recalled. Here again there is a fine line between two opposite kinds of retaliation.

The concept of the "wounded healer" is a corrective to the inherent imbalance of the power ratio in the therapeutic relationship. In his book *Is Human Forgiveness Possible?* (1987) John Patton writes, "I am more like those who have hurt me than different from them". It is equally possible to say: "As a therapist I am more like my client than different from my client". But such thinking is not always easy to comprehend: are the abused more like their abusers than different from them? The parallels are not immediately obvious, although the wish for revenge frequently gives rise to the criticism (uttered too often by those who have not experienced abuse) that "In wanting revenge you are making yourself just like them". There is little that can be said to such a comment other than "Yes", although to think revenge is not the same as to act it.

In summary, phrases like the "wounded healer", or "forgive and forget", or even "it is good to talk about your wish for revenge" are not as straightforward as we might wish them to be. The motives for caring through being a therapist include less obvious feelings, which include the wish for revenge, which can take a constructive and a destructive form. Even forgiveness is not free from the possibility of revenge. Nothing is what it seems. Perhaps that is the way it is with the search for understanding: we just begin to imagine we have it in our grasp when knowledge itself appears to turn on us and takes its revenge. Feste says at the end of *Twelfth Night*, "The whirligig of time brings in his revenges" (5. 4. 374). Indeed, experience sometimes seems to suggest that life consists of a perpetual vendetta.

CHAPTER SIX

Parallel process: confirmation and critique

T eaching one of the first British university courses in psycho-dynamic supervision in 1990, my wife and I developed several seminar topics, of which this chapter was my most far-reaching, since, as I explain below, I stood firm against the tide that was then sweeping the practice and teaching of supervision, which wanted to seek out parallel process, and to overtly display it to (and sometimes, it seemed, to dazzle) the supervisee. In 1996 my paper was published in the then *Journal of Psychodynamic Counselling*. It is seldom referred to in the literature, as if my critique fell on deaf ears. I still think parallel process needs qualification!

*   *   *

Erik Erikson is reputed to have said that in his early days he cautiously put it to young people that they might hate their parents. Later, when his ideas had caught on, he had to suggest to young people that they might also like them! His experience illustrates the pendulum swing of ideas, where a particular concept becomes so fashionable that an alternative and more original concept appears to become redundant. This has clearly happened, at least in common usage, to other psychodynamic concepts. Countertransference, for example, was once felt to be a block to understanding, for which personal therapy was needed. It then (rightly although confusingly) became defined as a means of identifying, through the therapist's reactions, what the client might be projecting (although "projective identification" is also used, and is more readily distinguishable from the original meaning of countertransference). The danger is then that countertransference in its original meaning as a possible blind spot gets forgotten, in favour of everything being the client's unconscious doing. The pendulum may need to swing back again to restore the importance of the original meaning.

Then there is the predominance of "transference" over the real relationship between client and therapist. Sometimes it seems as if transference has become way of disclaiming both the power and the normal effects of the actual therapy relationship, and that a swing back to the reality of such feelings may not be altogether inappropriate.

In this chapter my concern is particularly about the way in which "parallel process" has become a mantra, cited in some cases in virtually every psychodynamic supervision session, as well as, amazingly, in the supervision jargon of not a few practitioners who are actually suspicious of psychodynamic theory and practice. When teaching over many years on a supervision course, my experience on several occasions was of "parallel process" being employed as a cover for the trainee supervisor's own mistakes and inappropriate handling of the session. Parallel process became like the child's secret friend: "It wasn't me; it was parallel process that led to that confusion between us, and the session going wrong."

It is often necessary to return to the origins of a concept to examine the difference that might have evolved between its original expression, and the way it is used later by people who have never looked at the original context. The dynamic of the supervisory process owes much to the development of the concept of the relationship between supervisor and supervisee in the writing of Harold Searles, particularly an essay in his *Collected Papers on Schizophrenia and Related Subjects*. It is difficult now to realize what a breakthrough paper Searles published in 1955 under the title "The informational value of the supervisor's emotional experiences" (1955, pp. 157–176). It was a breakthrough because he extended the content of supervision beyond technique and theory, and beyond an "intellectual discussion" between two or more people, to looking at the actual supervisory relationship as a way of understanding the therapist and client. Early in the paper he observes that it was a long-held view that there should be no emotional reactions in supervisor or student, "other than those of a friendly teacher-and-colleague variety" (*ibid.*, p. 158). Around the time that Searles was writing about his experience of supervision there was growing recognition of the type of feelings in supervisor or supervisee that could actually interfere with supervision, such as competitiveness; it was felt that the supervisor's capacity to see these at work through his or her own emotional reactions would make for a better supervisory process. This recognition was, therefore, similar to the recognition of the problems that could be caused in therapy by countertransference.

Searles wrote a second paper on supervision a few years later: "Problems of psycho-analytic supervision" (1962, pp. 584–604). In it he quotes Keiser (1956):

> The progress of the candidate is recognized by his greater ease and facility in presenting to the supervisor, a diminution of blocks to his listening, his acceptance of supervision, a sharpened capacity to observe, an awareness of his typical mistakes which he learns to avoid, and his application of well-timed interpretations. To this I would add lessened dependence on the supervisor and a greater assumption of responsibility towards his patient. [Searles, 1962, p. 596]

Searles comments that, if we view supervision simply as a learning situation, this is a good description of the progress of a student but that it misses the "subtle resonances to the progressing treatment situation" (*ibid.*). He does not deny that there are problems of this order within supervision, and agrees that it remains important for a supervisor to be alert for difficulties that can occur. But that is not the only way of understanding difficulties and disturbances that arise. Even where there has been acknowledgement of the value of exploring emotional reactions (such as competitiveness) in the supervisory relationship, Searles points out that this advance stops far short of his own conception, which is that

the supervisor experiences, over the course of a supervisory relationship, as broad a spectrum of emotional phenomena as does the
therapist or even the patient himself—although to be sure, the
supervisor's emotions are rarely as intense as those of the therapist,
and usually much less intense than those of the patient. [1955,
p. 158]

In the 1955 paper, he says that the relationship between supervisor
and supervisee reflects the relationship between therapist and
client, which in turn reflects the internal world (and perhaps the
external relationships) of the client.

This seems to me to be another example, although Searles does
not himself draw the parallel, of the idea of the "living laboratory",
a term first introduced by Freud as a way of describing both analysis, and the value of transference within it. The relationship
between the therapist and client, particularly when it intrudes upon
the process, is an indication of other relationships, often earlier
ones, in the client's experience. Similarly, Searles suggests that, if
the relationship between the two or more people in supervision is
"disturbed" by emotional reactions, this need not be felt to be anti-
educational, nor interrupting the learning in supervision. It is both
therapeutic and educational. Searles concentrates upon such disturbance of feelings on the part of the supervisor, but makes it clear
that the disturbance can equally be in the supervisee as well.

Although transference is the parallel that I draw, in fact it is
countertransference that is more relevant to understanding his idea.
The supervisor's emotional reaction to the supervisee (or countertransference), as it occurs from time to time, might provide clues to
what is going on in the therapy. There are, as I have pointed out, two
meanings of countertransference, distinguished by whether the
reaction is primarily located in the client or the therapist, but Searles
is not keen on separating the two meanings. Unresolved problem
areas in the supervisor's life probably do underlie the supervisor's
emotional reactions, at least to some extent. There have to be
partially unresolved issues in the supervisor, otherwise these reactions would not occur in so noticeable a fashion. Searles acknowledges, and, indeed, is not over-concerned, that self-awareness can
never be so complete as to free a therapist from such emotional
involvement, particularly when there is a high degree of anxiety in
the client (1955, p. 174).

The 1955 paper was obviously a strong influence upon Janet Mattinson's work, and her use of the term "mirroring". She took up Searles' work in her monograph *The Reflection Process in Casework Supervision* (1975), where she refers to his paper "Oedipal love in the countertransference" (1959), a paper which was published almost half-way between his two papers on supervision. She describes countertransference as:

> *an innate and inevitable ingredient, which is sometimes a conscious reaction to the observed behaviour of the client, or which is sometimes an unconscious reaction to the felt and not consciously understood behaviour of the client, and which can be used for increased understanding of the client.*

> And with reference to Searles, I am also concerned with a fourth aspect: *the resolution by the worker of the counter-transference as one of the main ingredients of casework which enables the client to resolve and relinquish the transference.* [Mattinson, 1975, p. 35, original italics]

Searles believes that these reactions are "highly informative reflections of the relationship between the therapist and patient" (1955, p. 158). He suggests that the reflection process takes place partly because the supervisor is at a greater emotional distance from the patient than the therapist. In the 1962 paper, Searles writes,

> My potential usefulness springs in large part from the simple fact that I am at a greater psychological distance than is the student from the patient's psychopathology—specifically from the patient's anxiety and ambivalence. This greater distance leaves me *relatively* free from anxiety and able, therefore, to think relatively clearly and unconstrictedly. This position is mine, and this potential usefulness is mine, irrespective of whether, for example, in other situations the student may prove himself more intelligent than I, and a more effective practitioner than I. [1962, p. 587, original italics]

This passage, together with others in the same paper, indicate that Searles eschews a superior position as a supervisor. The relationship is not that of master and apprentice. Supervision works because the emotional atmosphere between supervisor and therapist is less intense than that in the therapist–client relationship, which in turn is less intense than in the client. Searles adds that the client, because of this, has the least capacity for self-awareness: it is this lack that partly brings the client to seek therapy. While it is the supervisor who should have the greatest capacity for self-aware-ness, the position of the supervisor, in terms of distance from the client, can be more in touch than the therapist is capable of being with her or his own unconscious, and with her or his emotional reactions, however bizarre. Searles cannot explain these phenom-ena, although he believes they are triggered by unconscious identi-fication.

He gives some examples, both from individual and from group work, listed below.

1. Searles started to supervise a therapist whose work he respected, but was surprised in the first supervisory hour to hear the therapist describing what was poor technique with the patient, which the therapist felt to be poor, too. While he described the incident, the therapist looked at Searles search-ingly, as though expecting criticism, and indeed he got it, because Searles felt it and expressed it. Searles was especially troubled when the second hour contained a detailed descrip-tion of another situation with the same patient, which was clearly anti-therapeutic. Searles again felt strong condemnation of the therapist, and began to wonder whether he could go on with the supervision if he was going to have these strong feel-ings of antipathy. He was just thinking this when the therapist told him that one of the things he noticed about his patient was that he kept presenting material which might be called ugly—perverse sexual material, things about faeces, etc., and how the patient, in presenting this, looked searchingly at the therapist. Searles was then able to point out the similarity between the therapist's reporting to him, and the patient's reporting to the therapist, and that it was perhaps a way of trying to maintain a distance between himself and the therapist.

2. After several months of supervision, a therapist was quoting the patient and the material was, as usual, quite confusing. As the therapist spoke, Searles fantasized the therapist asking for a declaration of love by Searles towards him. He dismissed this as irrelevant, only a few minutes later to hear him quote the patient as saying something that sounded like the disguised

expression of romantic love for her therapist. Searles' own reaction minutes before had enabled him to spot this, and suggest an interpretation, which enabled the sexual nature of the transference–countertransference situation to become clearer.

Without acknowledging his own fantasy to himself, he too might have missed the patient's reference, just as the therapist had done. He observes that it is not just negative feelings that are carried over into the supervisory process. He gives the example of a supervisor feeling especially fond of a therapist during a particular phase of their work, and that this in turn might be traceable to the current fondness patient and therapist have for each other.

3. He also gives examples from group supervision: where the members of the group reflected the relationship between thera-pist and patient, for instance, feeling very sleepy just as the therapist felt sleepy; or where the members of the supervision group failed to understand one another, and reflected the sense of disintegration in the patient being described.

In his 1962 paper, Searles also observes that, as the therapist–supervisor relationship changes for the better, so, too, does the client–therapist relationship; there is a type of two-way process:

> Supervision early involves an inarticulate kind of competition as to which of the two participants is to be the therapist for the other; subsequently, as the tensions in the relationship diminish and as the mutual and more explicit work concerning the patient proves increasingly successful, there develops an increasingly free give-and-take at this deeper level also. [1962, p. 601]

He has no doubt, therefore, that supervision can be therapeutic:

> I strongly surmise that we are moving towards the day when there will be . . . general agreement as to the essentially therapeutic significance, for both participants, of psycho-analytic supervision. Such a realization will require us to discover that *any* human inter-action which is at all intense and prolonged is, in a very real sense of the word *mutually* therapeutic (or anti-therapeutic). [*ibid.*, pp. 602–603, original italics]

The possibility of supervision being anti-therapeutic is worth pursuing. If the benefits of this kind of supervision are transferred back into the therapy itself, this can also happen where there are difficulties in the supervisory relationship. In the 1955 paper, Searles indicates that if there is more anxiety in the therapist–supervisor relationship than in the therapeutic relationship, this, too, can get transferred into the therapist–client relationship, and this then give rises to disturbing processes. Consider, then, that if there are disturbing reactions in supervision, this may be because what the therapist reports as happening in the original therapy is in fact a reflection of the supervisory relationship.

In making this point Searles is, therefore, suggesting that there are other ways of understanding parallel process—that it may be nothing to do with the original therapy being reported, but more to do with what is happening in supervision. This is one of several qualifications that Searles makes. It is echoed by Langs, who "suggests that the supervisor should hear the patient's comments as first potentially referring to himself (i.e. the supervisor), next to the therapist and only then as the patient talking about himself or others". This is quoted by Jones (1989), who draws upon Langs' work (1979), and himself provides an example of a patient's comments about being bruised, which could be taken as a reference to the way that Jones, as a supervisor, had tried to pressure a therapist over her handling of the patient's lateness (1989, p. 509).

I would add to Langs' observation, that the supervisor should also consider the *therapist's* comments as first potentially referring to the supervisory relationship, next to the therapist–client interaction, and only then to the client talking about him or herself and others. I can illustrate this from a supervision session with an experienced therapist, who was talking about her client being persistently late. The client had been so ever since a recent session in which the therapist felt the client had gone much deeper into her feelings than before, feelings about her dying partner. But the therapist had found herself very angry with the client for being late. She was fuming during the minutes she was kept waiting, thinking she could be doing something better with her time—that, indeed, she could be visiting another of her clients who was in hospital. For a while in the session we concentrated upon the session where her client had gone much deeper into her feelings about her partner.

The therapist had encouraged this. So we looked together at how the therapist might pull her own relationship with her client back in, rather than concentrate, as she had been, on interpreting the client's material as purely referring to her dying partner. The client's references to the poison in the atmosphere could, of course, be interpreted as the poison in her partner's body, but I thought that it was also about the poison that the client felt the therapist had introduced into the therapeutic relationship when she had encouraged the client to go deeper into her most painful feelings. I was about (à la Langs) to suggest to the therapist that it was important to start with the therapist–client references: only when those interpretations had been correctly made, and the client's relationship with the therapist had been rendered less dangerous, could the therapist again try to help the client reach into her painful feelings about her partner's inevitable death. Then I realized, while starting to say this, that there was this other layer that Langs referred to—that reports of the therapy session might refer to supervision. I suddenly saw how the therapist's anger with the lateness of her client might as much be possibly related to the fact that *I too* had been late—in fact, I had forgotten, and then turned up late for our previous appointment, one which we had had to move to a different day and time. I therefore made reference to my lateness, and wondered how much the therapist's anger with her client, which she admitted herself was over the top, was also anger with me for being late. The therapist responded by saying that we could all make mistakes, and that she forgot about sessions from time to time too, and therefore understood (which indeed she had said to me at the time). But she went on that she would have been very angry indeed if I had not turned up at all, because she was desperate to talk about the client she had just referred to as being in hospital. She had been desperately worried at how to handle that visit. That I had come in late, and we had three-quarters of the time left, had rescued the situation, but it still left its residue of anger with me for keeping her in suspense. It also made some sense of her opening remark in this particular supervision session, one of those casual asides that a supervisor might otherwise ignore, that she had that morning set her alarm clock wrong, and had arrived at her therapist's (whom she saw the hour before me) seventy-five minutes early.

Langs is, therefore, a counter-balance to Searles, or, more accurately, since Searles has made a similar point, to the pervasive idea that parallel process is all about what is going in the therapy as reflected in supervision. How the supervisor and supervisee feel, relate, and behave in the supervision might reflect the client. But, equally so, what the supervisee says about the client might reflect how the supervisee experiences the supervisor.

There follows another example, observed in a supervision training session.

Jill is supervising Jack. Jack starts by saying that he is getting nowhere with a bulimic client, and he is puzzled. Jill interrupts in the first minute and asks how Jack relates to the client, but Jack interrupts her by saying that the client had seen a counsellor before, but stopped after two sessions. He goes on to say how outwardly well adjusted the client appears, and how difficult it is to get beneath that.

Jill keeps quiet for a while, but interrupts again three minutes later when Jack talks about the client not coming to see him for a while; and Jack quickly in turn interrupts her, and talks about other breaks in the therapy. He says that part of him feels very irritated by the client. She talks and talks and he cannot say anything. About ten minutes later, during which time Jill has spoken briefly every minute or so, Jack says how every session with this client he attempts to stop her talking so much. She fills the session and keeps him at a distance. "I let her control me by her incessant talking," he says. Jill wonders whether he could stop the client, and focus on something. The supervision session goes on. Jill intervenes every minute or two, looking at the way the client keeps missing sessions, and how the client is avoiding looking at herself. After about twenty minutes she says to Jack, "There's so much there—such a huge amount—and yet you're not given an opportunity. It must be frustrating." Jack says, "Well, in her sweet way she puts me under tremendous pressure."

What is happening in this supervision session? Those who favour the use of parallel process at every turn may want to say that supervision is paralleling therapy, with the supervisor and the therapist interrupting each other, and perhaps the supervisor particularly identifying unconsciously with the client, so that it is actually difficult for Jack to get a word in edgeways. The supervisor fills the session, perhaps as the client also fills herself with food, and keeps Jack's case at a distance, as the client is keeping others at a distance. Alternatively, you could say that the supervisor, hardly before the session has got going, interrupts Jack, and that thereafter Jack talks about the client as breaking the therapy and not giving it a chance to work, because that is what the supervisor is doing to him. Certainly, many of the things that Jack says could just as well refer to the supervisor as to the client. In this particular session I think my preference is to accept Langs' interpretation of what is going on, rather than a potentially reflective process à la Searles.

As I have already indicated, Searles is also cautious about the process of reflection, something that has been overlooked, if indeed it was ever recognized, by those who have seized upon the parallel process without reading the original paper. His observation that what the therapist reports by way of interactions with the patient might, in fact, be a reflection of the supervisory relationship is only one of several cautionary notes about his hypothesis.

Searles does not concentrate upon overt feelings, but on picking up clues that might point to unconscious material, as yet perhaps not seen either by the client or the therapist, and only dimly or quickly glimpsed by the supervisor. Too often, parallel process is used to describe things that are staring the supervisory pair in the face. There is little subtlety about it as there is in Searles. In practice, too, we must note that such perceptions occupy only a small part of supervisory hours, although when they do occur they can offer clues to obscure yet highly relevant areas which trouble the therapeutic relationship. Parallel process does not occur all the time. Another caution should be noted in how Searles uses his emotional reactions: "Incidentally", he writes, "I am not advocating the supervisor's emoting, in an overt fashion, to the supervisee. I am focusing upon the supervisor's 'subjective' emotional experience in the supervisory situation" (1955, p. 158n). The following is an example of his proper reticence about what he is thinking and feeling. Writing of his approach to supervision, he adds, "These things I do not say to him [the therapist], rather they are implicit in the spirit with which I respond to him" (1962, p. 585).

It is difficult, therefore, to imagine that Searles would say, as I have heard several trainee supervisors say, "Ah, this is parallel process". Rather, he would store away his feeling until, as in therapy itself, there is some other communication that provides confirmation that his reaction might be relevant. Even then he would probably not refer to his own private reaction.

Finally, Searles makes it quite clear towards the end of his 1955 paper that the supervisor still has to consider whether there may be some other explanation for his emotional reactions; for example, the supervisor may be projecting an important part of his own personality on to both therapist and the client, and, not unnaturally, seeing a parallel, whereas in each case what he sees belongs to him rather than to each of them. Bearing in mind the closeness between disturbances in the supervisor and countertransference that I referred to earlier, Searles also points to the possibility that the phenomena he describes, of supervision apparently mirroring therapy, might sometimes be a form of classical countertransference in which the therapist responds to the patient and supervisor alike in the same way, so that, not surprisingly, there is a parallel process, but nothing to do with the patient.

Having reached this point it would not be surprising if the reader feels confused, and rightly so, because there are a large number of explanations for what is experienced in supervision. If I have the permutations right, we have to consider that, as the supervisor listens to the therapist describing the session with the client, what the supervisor experiences may be:

- what the therapist feels with the client;
- what the client feels with significant others;
- what the therapist feels with significant others;
- what the client feels with the therapist;
- what the therapist feels with the supervisor;
- what the supervisor feels with the therapist;
- what the supervisor feels with significant others.

No wonder Zinkin (rather unoriginally) calls supervision "the impossible profession" (1988). He reminds us that, strictly speaking, supervision cannot take place without sitting in the room while therapy and counselling is going on. Not even audio- or video-recording solves the problem, because any other outside factor alters what goes on. We might also add that even the thought of the supervisor in the therapist alters what is going on. Zinkin suggests in the end that supervision is actually a "shared fantasy". It is what results from the therapist sharing what he or she imagines the therapist and client have been doing together, and from the supervisor trying to imagine it too. As the supervisor listens, what he or she selects out is his or her interpretation of what the therapist is saying, which in turn is the therapist's own selective interpretation of what the client has been saying, which in turn is the client's own selective interpretation of what has been happening. We cannot ever know what is true. It would be easy to read Zinkin as either somewhat too clever or too cynical when he concludes his paper with the statement that supervision "works best if both remain aware that what they are jointly imagining is not true" (1988, p. 24). He adds, however, "there is teaching and learning to be found in this joint imaginative venture as there is in therapy itself" (*ibid.*).

But Zinkin does not say enough about what that learning is. Perhaps this is where Searles throws light on the impossibility of objective learning, because he suggests the possibility that, through the fantasies, imaginings, and intuitions that the supervisory relationship gives rise to, the supervisor is able partially to enter the fantasy world of the therapy itself. Through occasionally and partially perceiving the intuitive, imaginative world of the therapist, the supervisor is perhaps partially able to share in the imaginative, intuitive, interpretative world in which the client has her or his being.

Supervision is not always about parallel process. The possibilities of meaning that lie in the supervisor's and supervisee's informational experiences deserve greater attention if we are to save ourselves from the arrogance of thinking we have got unconscious processes well and truly taped!

CHAPTER SEVEN

Seeing and being seen

T his chapter was originally a lecture delivered at the request
of the Bath Centre for Counselling and Psychotherapy, at a
time when I was their external moderator. Subsequently, I
was made an emeritus life member, and have valued the link with
that prestigious training centre. The subject was requested, and like
all such requests, entailed some research into the literature on what
emerged as a fascinating topic. It subsequently appeared as an article in the *European Journal of Psychotherapy, Counselling and Health.* I
delivered the paper to one or two other groups, and, like all such
occasions in my experience, generated interesting conversations
afterwards that added considerably to my own understanding of
the subject. As acknowledged in the original paper when
published, I am grateful to Ruth Jones, a registered art therapist, for
permission to use her observations and analysis of the stages of
seeing and being seen, and to colleagues and supervisees for
permission to use examples from their practice.

*   *   *

There are some aspects of counselling and psychotherapy that
appear so obvious that they are beyond question. Recognition of

non-verbal communication is one of them, explained and illustrated in all the basic books on listening, responding, and therapeutic communication as one of the foundation skills. While it is
undoubtedly the case that therapists and counsellors learn to moni-
tor their client's and their own non-verbal communication, there
are, in fact, more facets to this than basic training can cover, with
subtleties of communication that carry various types of significance. The purpose of this chapter is to focus on one particular form
of non-verbal communication, that of seeing and being seen, and, if
it might be put this way, to take a closer look at it. It needs to be
emphasized at the start that I recognize that visually impaired therapists or clients may have different experiences from those
described below, which I have not been able to include but would
of course be of great interest to sighted therapists and counsellors.

A familiar cartoon about psychoanalysis is that of a patient lying
on a couch, with a bearded and bespectacled analyst sitting behind
the patient's head writing notes. In fact, Freud's advice to budding
analysts was *not* to write notes, because to do so would distract
them from attending to the patient. Nevertheless, in other respects
such cartoons accurately portray the scene they wish to poke fun at.
The couch (although Freud never used that term and only ever
refers to the sofa) encouraged relaxation on the part of the patient.
It was a throwback to Freud's period of experimentation with hyp-
nosis, and continued to assist dream-like free association in the
patient. Sitting out of sight was felt to assist a parallel attitude in the
analyst of free-floating attention, and additionally served Freud's
purpose because "he did not want his patients to watch his facial
expression, lest they be unduly swayed by his responses" (Gay,
1988, p. 296). Such apparently objective a justification for what we
now understand as "the blank screen" technique in psychoanalysis
(or "mirror", as Freud actually calls it, a term returned to in a more
direct sense below) might, however, mask more subjective reasons
for Freud's staying out of sight. One biographer quotes him as
saying, "I cannot stand being stared at eight hours a day (or longer)
by others".

In adopting this physical positioning, even though it did not
totally remove the physical expression of the patient from Freud's
sight, a very significant shift was made in terms of the therapeutic
approach. As Roudinesco (1990) makes clear in her magisterial

study of the development of psychoanalysis in France, traditional medicine relies upon *visual* evidence, and upon a thorough examination, partly through touch, but mainly through *sight* of the patient's body. This remains just as true in the high-tech medicine of our own time, with its use of X-rays, scans, and fibre optics, delivering clear pictures of the organs and pathways of the human body. The visual method of examination at one time also pertained to psychiatry: an example of this can be seen in Roudinesco's description of one of Lacan's mentors, Clérambault (after whom the syndrome is named which describes obsessive erotic attachments and "stalking"). Clérambault was a theoretician of erotomania and an expert in the mechanics of paranoia. Roudinesco calls him "the master of the gaze" (*ibid.*, p. 108), describing his method as "tyrannical", seeking out the symptoms and proving the coherence of his theory before worrying about the patient. She continues her description, "He spent his life perfecting his eagle-eye gaze; he manipulated and observed his patients without ever listening to them" (*ibid.*, p. 106). What is also interesting is that in his private life he had a "passion for fabrics, hems, pleats, ruffles, in a word the fetishized love of the adorned body of the (preferably Arab) female" (*ibid.*, p. 108); he kept wax figurines, which he draped with clothes. So the gaze, for Clérambault, had both a professional and a personal force. Ironically, perhaps even tragically, Clérambault went blind and he committed suicide. As Roudinesco observes, "the master of the gaze could not bear to lose his sense of relief, color, and perspective" (*ibid.*, p. 109).

Medicine was, and in some cases remains, more concerned with seeing and with the evidence of the eye, than it is with hearing and the evidence disclosed to the ear. Therapists have pointed out this weakness in much of the training of doctors, and their subsequent failure to listen. Yet Clérambault influenced the young Lacan, even if he added to his own approach that method which Freud had earlier been forced by one of his patients to adopt, that of listening. Roudinesco writes of Lacan,

> If he made use essentially of the psychoanalytic method, he would never give precedence to the ear at the expense of the eye. His tendency was rather to integrate a listening to the subject and a visual observation of his person. [*ibid.*, p. 122]

The physical examination of psychotherapy patients has, quite rightly, been separated out from psychological assessment in the development of analytic technique. This separation has perhaps meant a failure to appreciate the significance of embodiment, even though there is clear evidence (e.g., McDougall, 1989) of a revival of interest in the somatic half of the psychosomatic equation. What Freud initially was able to combine as both a physician and an analyst, that is, physical as well as psychoanalytical examination, he later had to caution his pupils against. In another generation, as a paediatrician Winnicott also remained free in his Paddington Green clinic to combine these two ways of using his senses. The physical examination of the children in hospital practice was a joy to him: he valued the bodies of children as well as their minds. As one of his former colleagues told me about Winnicott's work, "Most of the therapy is being seen by somebody, examined by somebody, finding the body beautiful". There is, however, a question in physical medicine of whether the child or adult patient feels embodied or disembodied by the type of gaze that comes from the eyes of the doctor.

The question of the relative weight to be attached in psychotherapy to the eye and the ear is a fascinating one. Lacan may have valued the visual as much as listening, but even he proposes that it is not until the advent of language that the infant can realize the object of the infant's gaze. Generally, in the development of psychotherapeutic technique the importance of the gaze has become diminished. Yet, there is more to seeing and being seen than the observation of non-verbal communication. The latter is a limited aspect of the total engagement with the client, whereas in the whole process of seeing and being seen there is a continuous metaphor for the progress of the therapeutic relationship.

I suspect that most psychotherapy has opted for the primacy of the word. Psychotherapy has, of course, been dubbed "the talking cure": it cannot take place without words. The ear is essential, and if hearing is impaired, there must be alternative means of communicating speech: lip-reading, sign language, etc. While it is possible to envisage with little difficulty a visually impaired therapist, it is difficult to imagine a hearing impaired therapist who does not have signing, lip-reading, or some other means of "listening" to the client. Nevertheless, what we hear, on its own, is liable to be dry, conceptual, and dull, except when word pictures make for more engaging communication. In the psychodynamic approach, and in many humanistic therapies, therapists and counsellors value imagery and the symbolic as a vital part of the verbal communication.

What we hear is often turned in our imagination into the visual: in the communication that takes place in therapy words are used to translate what has been seen in the mind's eye of the client to the mind's eye of the therapist and back again. The way I use "visual" here is, of course, as metaphorical as the term "the mind's eye", and the terms "insight" or "imagination". Here, however, in concentrating upon the importance of sight, I am more concerned with the literal act of looking, and the significance of the gaze.

Continuing in the tradition of Clérambault and Lacan, and referring back to Freud's theory of sexual drives, there are some interesting parallels in French psychoanalysis that are drawn between therapy, voyeurism, and the cinema. Metz's definitive study of *Psychoanalysis and Cinema* is written from a Lacanian perspective. He points out that "psychophysiology makes a classic distinction between 'senses at a distance' (sight and hearing) and the others all of which involve immediate proximity and which it calls the 'senses of contact'" (1982, p. 59), such as touch, taste, smell, etc. Freud (1905a), too, notes that there is a difference between the various expressions of sexual drives, for example, the desire to see (voyeurism and scopophilia—scopophilia is the wish to see) differs from orality. In voyeurism the object of the drive (the person being looked at) and the source of the drive (the eye that looks) are always kept apart. But in orality, for example, the object needs to enter the mouth, to make contact, even to be consumed, for the same pleasure to be found. This question of distance and space is one that is profoundly important in relation to seeing and being seen as an expression of the quality of the psychotherapeutic relationship.

The "senses at a distance", as distinct from the "senses of contact", are two-fold: the eye and the ear. The primacy of the eye in Freud's treatment of drives or impulses should not blind us to similar qualities in hearing. Lacan includes it as one of the four main sexual drives, and the possible eroticization of hearing should not be forgotten, even though it is given no further attention here. I concentrate upon the scopophilic drive.

Freud devotes more attention to the desire to see than he does to the other "sense at a distance", the desire to hear. When we look back to Freud, as early as *Three Essays on Sexuality* in 1905, where he locates the love of looking, scopophilia, he does not confine it to a perversion. He does not use the term in a pejorative sense, as we may be tempted to do when we refer to "voyeurism". He refers to the pleasure in looking as part of the natural progression towards sexual fulfilment. Visual excitation is the most frequent pathway to libidinal excitement, and natural selection has in many cases favoured the development of beauty with that in mind. It is usual for most people, he writes, to linger on any looking which has a sexual tone to it. Nevertheless, looking can also be sublimated—he cites the arts as shifting away from the genitals to the body as a whole, so directing part of libidinal desire to higher aims (Freud, 1905a, pp. 156–157). He perhaps indulges in a little of his own titillation when he asserts that "the progressive concealment of the body that goes along with civilization keeps sexual curiosity awake" (1905a, p. 156), but he only refers to looking as becoming a perversion when it fails to progress towards sexual fulfilment. There is not as yet in those early essays any close link (such as later psychopathology might make) between voyeurism, or its opposite form, exhibitionism, and castration anxiety about the lost penis, although Freud perhaps comes close to this idea when he suggests that sexual curiosity seeks to complete the sexual object by revealing its hidden parts.

In referring to "scopophilic drive", "castration anxiety", and "voyeurism" in association with the act of seeing, I may appear to espouse these older Freudian drive and sexuality theories, when current psychoanalytic thought prefers object relations theory. Drive theory can, nevertheless, be translated so it does not have to be seen *purely* in terms of genital sexuality. For sexual drive we might substitute "the wish to love and be loved", while not forgetting that for some people this wish seems only to be expressed in sexual terms. Seeing and being seen might then relate to this wish to love and to be loved, to connect and to be connected with the other. Alongside this wish there may also arise many different types of fear, including castration anxiety, which, translated into object relations theory, might also be anxiety about loss or about the lost object.

Looking, then, is a part of relating, intimate relating, which includes sexual relating, although it is not confined to genitality. Seeing and being seen may involve castration anxiety, especially if that term can be taken as referring more generally to the lost object. Metz observes, following Lacan, that the sexual drives, which include seeing and hearing, always remain more or less unsatisfied, even when their object has been attained (1982, p. 59). Desire is quickly reborn after it has been satisfied; it has no real object, because all its objects are substitutes. Desire "pursues an imaginary object (a 'lost object') which is its truest object, an object that has always been lost and is always desired as such" (*ibid.*). Looking might then include desire for the lost object, which might be a part object, such as (but not confined to) the breast or the penis, or may be a whole object relation.

To recapitulate, there is a difference between the visual and auditory drives and the other drives. The visual and the auditory, "the senses at a distance", always have space between them and their object. Metz points out that

> it is no accident that the main socially acceptable arts are based on the senses at a distance, and that those which depend on the senses of contact are often regarded as "minor" arts (e.g. the culinary arts, the art of perfumes, etc.). [*ibid.*]

It may be no accident that what is ethically acceptable in the practice of therapy is relationship through the visual and the auditory. The other senses (touch, smell, and taste) carry more risks, because their functioning leads to a type of closeness that is generally not acceptable in the therapeutic relationship. Their expression might even constitute acting out.

In referring above to Clérambault's personal erotomania, or, as Roudinesco also calls it, his "love of draping", I did so not out of salaciousness, but to illustrate the importance of looking, not just as represented in traditional medical examination and diagnosis, but also in psychopathology, and obviously I am suggesting a link between the two. Therapists might like to draw upon the visual appearance of their clients in detecting underlying and possibly repressed emotions, but they look in other ways, too: their work inevitably involves a degree of voyeurism. We might say, then, that a therapist is permitted to be a voyeur, albeit a registered or accredited voyeur, and that the client is allowed and encouraged to be an exhibitionist. These active and passive forms of scopophilia, to which Freud draws our attention in *Three Essays on Sexuality*, are part of the therapeutic alliance. Active and passive scopophilia are also part of the experience of cinema, the study of which has drawn considerably upon psychoanalysis. Metz observes how important it is (and readers will be familiar with this themselves when entering an almost empty cinema) to sit in the right place. Cinema spectators take care to avoid being too close to or too far from the screen (*ibid.*, p. 60). Voyeurism, and indeed exhibitionism, necessitates a space between the object and the eye. The space represents both the dissatisfaction of never being able to reach the object, yet also the satisfaction of being at the right distance, a distance that, for the pleasure of voyeurism, must not be filled in (*ibid.*).

The importance of space might suggest how important it is in seeing and being seen that the therapist and client adopt the right distance from each other. There are a number of reasons for this, not least that the therapist represents the lost object, and remains the lost object. Therapy might be said to be, to employ a phrase that Metz uses of all desire, including voyeurism, "the infinite pursuit of [the] absent object". Bridging that gap, which, of course, touch may attempt to do, suggests the illusion that the lost object can be grasped. But the lost object cannot be so grasped, just as in our verbal communication there will always be gaps (seen, for example, in Bion's concept of not-knowing, and Winnicott's concept of True Self as that which is never known, even to ourselves).

What are the implications for therapy of the recognition of both desire and anxiety, of the wish for closeness and yet the need for distance, in seeing and being seen? There is a tradition of watchfulness in psychoanalysis, as Peter Lomas says in a videotape conversation, that can inhibit clients. Psychoanalysis and psychotherapy, he says, is a very watchful process: the client is under scrutiny. He cites evidence that it is not good for a child to be continuously watched, or not to be given space (Lomas & Jacobs, 1991). The following examples show how this might occur in practice.

An analyst has recorded an example of transference that also illustrates the significance of seeing and being seen. I summarize and quote the analyst's description.

Mr T arrived on time for his session, and as he came into the room he looked at me briefly, but piercingly, before looking away at his feet. He then looked back at me, his eyes widened and he said, challengingly, "What?" For a moment I felt afraid I could be attacked by him physically.

I said nothing, but when he was lying on the couch, looking tense and suspicious, I told him he had felt that I had been looking at him in what had felt like a bad way. He remained silent. I added that he had thought something had happened in that look. He scratched the inside of one nostril, quite violently, and then replied that I had seemed to "look into him". I said I thought he had felt my look as something that had penetrated him—got right up his nose and irritated him in a sensitive place somewhere inside him. He snorted, saying, "Of course, I don't know what goes on in your head, and I know you will never tell me. I know how you people are trained. You'd be in trouble if you told me what you really thought." He then looked acutely worried and "explained" himself by saying he had meant "trouble with other analysts". It was clear he meant more senior analysts, in a super-egoish way.

The analyst felt that Mr T's fear of his analyst's looking was being experienced as "a shoving right back into him of whatever he had looked into me as he came into the room, before he had looked at his feet". This led to a very important dream in which the analyst was able to look at some of the paranoid transference in the patient towards his analyst. He goes on:

Mr T had left the previous day feeling angry and dismissed, following a session in which he had felt understood by me. The look he gave me today did not seem reproachful, but felt almost like a stab, and it was swiftly followed by his paranoid feeling of my looking penetratingly back at him. I felt he had projected into me something violent and intrusive from himself, possibly associated with his having felt dismissed and ejected by me the following day when he had been feeling close to me. Having done this, he'd felt he had to look quickly away, and I think this may have been because he had not wanted to see what his projection had done to me, and also he may already have felt afraid of me retaliating in kind . . . His "What?" had the quality for me, in my countertransference, of being like on the receiving end of a bar-room confrontation—"You looking at me?!"

When he remained silent, I added simply a comment to the effect that looking was not experienced as just looking, but that something was felt to have happened. In other words, that he was in a state of mind in which what went on between us were actions, not communications. His response to this was itself an action, not a verbal thought. I took his nose picking as a communication of his feeling that my look, and possibly now my words, is an intrusion into him, attacking him in a sensitive, vulnerable place. [Private communication.]

This example starts with an actual look, which then gets translated into the symbolic significance of the look, although the look is also a way of symbolically stating the anxiety of the patient. It is interesting to relate the paranoid experience of this patient (and, indeed, at one stage paranoia in the analyst too, thinking that the patient was going to throw something at him) to the power of the look, as in the concept of the evil eye, or in the conviction of being watched as in paranoid delusions.

It may not be insignificant that Erikson has identified the numinous and the act of looking or being looked upon with the first age of trust. Erikson illustrates the act of looking in the rituals of religious ceremonies: for example, in the elevation of the host in the Mass, or in the use of sacred icons and images. This sense of the numinous is closely linked by Erikson to the relationship between mother and baby, which also involves gazing, responding to, and being looked at and smiled upon (Capps, 1983). It is in seeing and being seen that a baby is helped to overcome her fear of separation and isolation. In religion, too, although the numinous in one sense suggests a distance between the worshipper and the god, it is the numinous aspect of ritual that also helps to overcome a person's sense of isolation from their god. Erikson also describes a more negative form of this, which he calls "ritual excess", idolatry, the reverse side of the numinous. Although Erikson refers to idolatry in religious terms, with objects being treated like gods, an equivalent idolatry is present in human relationships, where it is also known in psychological terms as idolizing or idealizing. The reverse side of idealization is not just denigration, but also paranoid fear of the idealized object. It may be that Mr T in one session idealized his analyst, then felt rejected, so that the idealization turns to paranoia.

Other examples illustrate the anxiety, perhaps paranoid anxiety, of being looked at by the therapist. Two clients described to me in supervision each used a number of verbal devices to avoid being too closely scrutinized. The first was a woman whose conversation was very intellectual. There was one particular moment of break-through when the therapist suggested that the client might try an imaginative exercise. She recommended that both the client and herself close their eyes for it. The client's intellectualism was put to one side, and much more graphic descriptions followed, which were expressed with real feeling. It appears that it was not seeing or not being seen that helped this to occur (similar, of course, to Freud's recommendation of the couch to block eye contact). In another example, a male client spoke very fully, but always about surface issues. His rapid delivery prevented the therapist from getting too close. His verbal gymnastics were accompanied by look-ing up into the air, or looking through partially closed eyes, leading the therapist to wonder whether there was a wish not to be seen. This was partially confirmed by the way he described himself as hiding beneath the bedclothes when depressed, for as much as a week at a time. There may have been some connection here to the sexual exposure to which he had been subjected by his father when he was a child, although to broach such a possibility with him was at that stage, when he expressed such reservations about seeing and being seen, to risk coming too close.

Another example of seeing and being seen in therapy demon-strates a similar anxiety as well as a diametrically different phase. Gail Yariv (1993), in a paper on the fear of being seen, describes the case of one of her clients, a young man who could not look at her at all; it took many months before he could do so. She describes how one day "his eyes locked into mine with a fierce and desper-ate glare that never shifted and never blinked" (ibid., p. 143). She describes her response to this, that "over the next few years I held his gaze". Only after some years (this was long-term therapy) was he able to let go his gaze and look away and then back again, as in more normal eye contact.

When I first read this case I had the mistaken impression that the therapist, by her gaze, had responded to her client in precisely the way Lomas says should be avoided, and that her watchfulness was excessive. I imagined that this situation was perilously like those that therapists will have encountered, where a potential duel through the power of the gaze seems to be sought by the client. In such circumstances the client locks her or his eyes on to the therapist and virtually stares the therapist out. That has always seemed to me to be a way of trying to keep the therapist at a distance.

I might not have known the precise circumstances of Yariv's case, since articles cannot go into too much detail, but in a private communication she made it clear to me that in this case her client could not bear her looking away, although she initially tried to do this. If she let go his gaze it felt to him as if she was dropping him into an abyss. While there was rage and hate in the gaze, there was also fear and desperation. Perhaps there *was* an element of the challenge to a duel, if only to try to prove that the therapist would not contain him, although the therapist thinks not. Yariv reports that when she was able to look and look away, like a mother with her baby, as indeed her client eventually was able to do, this was a real achievement in the therapy. Without having the experience of being with this client, I can only speculate on how closely this shift in the client's and therapist's gaze took place as a result of subtle mirroring between the two. In the article Yariv rightly acknowledges different aspects of sight: the fear of being seen, the wish to be recognized, and the fear of the all-seeing therapist. Those who are interested in integrating the significance of sight and blindness in mythology with client material will find much richness in her paper.

My correspondence with Yariv led me to wonder whether other therapists had the experience I had certainly had with some of my clients, of being locked in what felt like a battle through the gaze. In a small poll of students and registered therapists, I found this was indeed the case: one therapist told me of an example where he felt distinctly pushed away by his female client's stare. As she told her history he realized why: she was a survivor of sexual abuse, and she not only needed to keep the therapist at a distance because he was a man, but also had to watch him like a hawk lest he provide any hint of threat toward her.

A caveat is necessary here. The type of eye contact that is considered appropriate between people in normal circumstances is often culturally determined. A German therapist commented to me, on Lomas's observation about watchfulness, that in her country they regard the British way of looking away as somewhat strange, since in Germany people look each other in the eye, and hold the gaze. A therapist brought up in the West Indies countered this by describing how, in her country of origin, looking down and not making eye contact is considered polite. She experienced the British gaze as staring, while her German colleague experienced it as shifty. Such cultural differences must also be borne in mind before too readily interpreting the gaze of our clients, or their response to our gaze.

It is important not to overlook the communication through the visual senses that takes place in some therapies through the use of art and through play. It is also present in Winnicott's practice of the Spatula Game and the Squiggle game. Yet, even here, there might be a particular significance in the act of looking and being seen. An art therapist, Ruth Jones, in some private communications on these matters, has made some valuable links to her work with children diagnosed with autism and communication disorders. I draw here directly from her correspondence.

Jones has found that the process of developing the possibility of a therapeutic relationship grows from the initial starting point of her own tentative seeing. She begins by working delicately with what she can see, which often at first sight may seem to be impenetrable behaviours and rituals. She tentatively gives verbal and other sound responses (noises, expression of pleasure, pain, shock—"ouch", "oh no", "oooh!") and physical responses (eyes, facial expression, gestures) to what she feels she might be seeing. She is describing at this stage solely her own capacity to see and make sense of what she might be observing. She is careful not to impose her "way of seeing", but rather communicates her interest in seeing what there may be to be seen (e.g., trying to make sense of the apparently random selection of colours a child was making from a pot of felt pens). The child begins to trust her ability to keep enough distance, so that he or she can begin to return and hold the therapist's regard. The child is slowly able to relax, at first periodically, as if trust ebbs and flows, to a time when he or she may be able to allow the therapist to interact more directly or even "help" (e.g., able to accept a pen from her when she has, apparently correctly, anticipated which colour they would use next). This is in conjunction with a mirroring verbalization of what the therapist can make sense of, of what is going on in front of her eyes. This seems to lead towards the possibility of the child also using language, verbalizations, sounds, and gestures towards her as the therapist/ person in relatedness.

Jones writes:

I have worked with a child who displayed astonishing diversity in
his levels of ability and development, who had verbal skills and
conceptual thinking far in advance of his years, but who was
emotionally very immature, unable to accept "help" and who was
unable to make any mark on paper, not writing nor drawing nor
scribble. In my work with him, when I found that his verbal "wild
goose chase" impaired my thinking and my ability to function as
an art therapist, I took the extreme step of putting my fingers in my
ears to remind both myself and him that I am an art therapist and
therefore primarily working with what is visible. This had a
profound and very positive impact on the course of the work with
the child, who understood that I understood when he was trying to
"dazzle" me or "create mirages" with his words. [Private communication.]

In the ongoing correspondence with me, Jones began to develop
a way of analysing the progression through which she and the child
come together in their work, which clearly also has relevant for
therapists working with adult clients who are deeply anxious or
unable to relate.

1. The child sees (i.e., scans) and the therapist sees, separately.
2. The child looks, the therapist looks, separately.
3. The child allows the therapist to look at them (allows her or
    himself to be seen).
4. The child allows the therapist to see them looking; the use of art
    materials kinetically (sensation).
5. The child and the therapist looking at (and into) each other.
6. Development of reciprocity, dialogue of looking, watching, and
    seeing.
7. The use of art materials symbolically (mark making); develop-
    ment of play.
8. The use of art materials for representative work (image
    making), development of language.

There is another aspect to the therapist's gaze that is distinct
from the actual experience of the visual. Illusion may seem far
removed from actual sight, although illusion can involve the visual,

as much as hallucinations seem to be perceived through the eyes. When a conjurer makes a coin disappear, or produces a rabbit out of a hat, it is our eyes that have seen this, even if we know in our minds that our eyes have also deceived us.

I refer here to a phenomenon of which I have become much more acutely aware in my practice, the visual perception of clients. I am not describing non-verbal communication in a client, such as what colours a client wears, or their actual appearance. In the instances I relate, from my own and from others' experience, the illusion is part of the countertransference perception, although apparently confirmed in its validity in other, more direct, expressions by the client.

A counsellor was relating in supervision how she had felt when she first met a male client whom she had so far seen for three sessions. The first thing that struck her about him when she met him in the waiting room was that his hair was dyed in streaks in two colours: the left side of his head was streaked signal red, and the right side of his head was bright green. The counsellor described in supervision how the client had been dismissive of the value of counselling in the first session, although she had worked hard to enable him to return for a second session. In that session he was much more forthcoming, and he related rather well to her. In the third session, the client was back to his more critical and rather belligerent state. What the counsellor had noticed, and felt was very curious, was that the first time she had met her client he had towered over her, larger than life and menacing. She had gone to the waiting room on the second occasion expecting to see the same man, but instead could only recognize him by the colour of his hair, because he was small, in fact shorter than her. She thought to herself, "I've completely forgotten what this client looked like— isn't he tiny?" It was in this session that the client was both vulnerable and co-operative, and made a closer relationship. And as the counsellor thought about it, she recognized that at the start of the third session she had fleetingly once again seen her client as large. That session was another distant and hostile one.

The counsellor had already linked this sharp divide in the two ways the client related to her to the two colours in his hair, as if he had one half of him which issued a warning signal, "Stop", and another which seemed to say "Go ahead". I said in response that compared to her account of how she had visually perceived her client, my own thoughts were rather insignificant. I had been wondering, as the counsellor described the sessions, which way the client's head had been turned to her: whether it was the red or the green side of the head that had faced her. I added that I had dismissed the thought because the client would not move the chair to allow this to happen. The counsellor said, with some amazement, that what I had said was interesting, because, as she thought about it now, in the first and third sessions the client had turned his head so that the red side faced her; and in the second session, when he was in her eyes smaller and more co-operative, he had indeed displayed the green side.

What a therapist can "see" in an illusory way might therefore be of some value. Another supervisee related to me that there are times in her sessions with a thirty-year-old woman client, severely emotionally deprived and abused as a child, when the therapist sees her as a gaunt and drawn woman; times when she looks more like a child; and times when she glimpses her as being a beautiful woman. Again, this is not simply non-verbal communication, nor is it an act on the part of the client; it is the way the therapist perceives the client.

Readers will be familiar with the point in therapy, particularly long-term therapy, where a client looks more assured, more person-able, or more attractive. This is similar to the phenomenon described by Searles in his paper on oedipal love in the countertransference (1965). My own experience with a client of such feelings seemed to have a totally different explanation to it. Tanya was a twenty-year-old student, daughter of parents who had divorced, her mother an actress, her father a failed businessman. She was academically bright, but lacked any core self-esteem, and spent most of the first three months' weekly sessions literally apologizing for herself. From time to time I caught glimpses of a more mature and attractive woman, and I had in those moments a sense of hope. After a further three months in which she became more settled and far less apolo-getic, she began to talk about a young man she had met, who clearly liked her. She did not know whether to tell her mother or father— her mother, she feared, would envy her daughter's opportunities and youth, and would denigrate her, as she had done at other times in her life. She thought her father might be pleased.

In the following session Tanya looked almost ugly to me. I found it difficult to believe that she was the same growingly attractive young woman I had been working with. She began to talk about her father, and how his response had been that he hoped very much that her relationship would not distract her from her degree, because it was her work that was the most important thing in her life. I began to realize that what I might be seeing was a type of spitting image of her father. Her face had appeared lined and masculine, and hence unattractive and unfitting upon her slim and youthful body. Later in the session, Tanya began to express her anger at her father's response, and to tell me instead how her mother had in fact been quite excited by her news. I thought then that Tanya's face changed as well. Now she was, in my illusion, the spitting image of her mother, or her mother when she was younger. I had not, of course, met either parent, and these were my own illusions, but I felt through them the powerfulness of her parents' opinions upon her, so that she almost wore their expression, their view of her rather than her own. She mirrored them.

I have concentrated to this point on how the therapist looks at and sees the client, although at times this seems closely linked to the way the client perceives the relationship with the therapist. Another aspect, which has received particular attention from Lacan, Winnicott, and Kohut, is the way a therapist provides a mirror for the client, as a mother provides a mirror in herself for her baby. Freud (1912e) uses the image of the mirror to indicate that the analyst shows nothing of himself, although in not being seen, as it were, holds a mirror up for the client to look into.

Seeing and being seen can have a rather more positive gloss. Winnicott writes, "the mother is looking at the baby and what she looks like is related to what she sees there" (1971, p. 112). His observation has been confirmed by simultaneous video studies of the faces of infants and their parents (including fathers), in which parent and child can be clearly seen to respond to each other: it is not simply that the baby responds to the mother's smile, but that the mother also mirrors her baby's expressions. In Kohut's identification of dimensions of the self he posits in the baby a "grandiose" self, developing from healthy infantile exhibitionism to mature self esteem, needing a response from mirroring (affirming) objects. The need for mirroring is mainly provided in therapy by the therapist's "empathic attunement", understanding how the client experiences himself, or herself, and others. Cartwright describes the Kohutian principle in this way:

> The empathically attuned therapist is sensitive not just to the way the patient feels, but also to the way he or she thinks, and the inter-relationships between different feelings and thoughts. The accuracy and quality of the therapist's attunement is central, providing a mirror to the patient of their whole self, including thoughts and feelings which are denied. [Cartwright, 1996, p. 39]

One way in which this mirroring is seen in therapy is the client's wish to identify with the therapist. This is sometimes based upon visual perceptions—on what we might almost call a "copy-cat" expression. A therapist reported in supervision how often her client, suffering low self-esteem following a bereavement, would say things to her like, "Look, I've got a ring just like that one you are wearing"; or "I've got a dress at home the same colour as yours". Another therapist described how one day she broke one of her contact lenses and wore her glasses in the session, something she had never done before with a particular male client. The next week he turned up wearing glasses, which he similarly had never done before. This physical identification is clearly based upon seeing and being seen, which itself may help affirm the self-esteem of the client (as well as the therapist, who might secretly enjoy being emulated).

Just as Jones (above) describes a progression in the way the relationship in art therapy builds up with an autistic child through seeing and being seen, there is also a progression in the way a client sees a therapist. There might, therefore, be stages of the mirroring process in therapy. I draw here upon the French psychologist Henri Wallon's study (1931) of the effect of mirror images, which itself inspired Lacan's work on the mirror stage (1949), to sketch what these might be.

Therapy often starts with an intensely inward-looking client, who sees very little of the therapist, either in fact or fantasy. For most clients, the initial containment of therapy allows them to dare to open their eyes and look around them. I had at one time a consulting room with a large poster of the Victoria Falls, directly facing the door. It was not an infrequent happening, around the third or fourth session, for a client to come through the door and say, "Oh, you have a new picture." In earlier sessions the picture had obviously not registered at all. But *they*, of course, had created a picture that they imagined had not been there before. This was their mirage, unknown to them, the result of their own omnipotent creation. It always seemed to me to be a sign that I, too, was being recognized as having some existence as well.

The next stage might be that described by Winnicott, writing of the infant looking at mother, but equally applicable to the client and the therapist:

> When I look I am seen, so I exist.
> I can now afford to look and see.
> I now look creatively and what I apperceive I also perceive.
> In fact I take care not to see what is not there to be seen (unless I am tired). [Winnicott, 1971, p. 114]

Then there might come a point when clients are able to recognize some of what they have not allowed themselves to see, reflected in the therapist, although at this stage with as yet a somewhat anxious smile on the client's part. Later, the client recognizes more of the self through the therapist, more confidently and willingly embracing what the therapist tries to offer back. There comes a time when there is a clearer distinction between the person of the therapist and the mirrored image of the client in the therapist, ending up in what I suggest might be the therapist reflecting the otherness of the client. Perhaps this is the point at which the therapeutic relationship might be said to be resolved and dissolved. In mapping such stages of therapy, it might be important to have a sense of how much clients are looking to see themselves, and also the point at which they are ready to see the separateness of the therapist.

I am unsure whether a satisfactory conclusion to therapy would include the recognition by the client that none of us ought to believe too literally in what we see; or whether it might be expressed in the famous words of the apostle Paul: "and then I shall know even also as I am known". It would be fitting if the client could see the therapist with greater clarity, less now "through a glass darkly" but more "now face to face" (I Corinthians 13: 12). Clients have their illusions of the therapist, and perhaps for the transference to be resolved they need to experience healthy disillusionment. It is not always flattering, even if it is more real. "I thought he was the handsomest man I ever saw," said one former patient, asked about her analyst in a study of the therapeutic relationship, "Then about a year after my therapy was completed, I saw him again, and realized that he was bald, grossly overweight, had bad skin, bad breath, and was a sloppy dresser. A caring, sensitive man, but nothing like what I had imagined. How could I not have seen that?" Perhaps it needs time before clients can see through the illusions they may have of the therapist.

In summary, seeing and being seen carries great significance. It is a living metaphor for the space, whether distant or close, between client and therapist, embodying key aspects of the client's ways of relating. The gaze of the therapist might be threatening or encouraging; the way the therapist is seen might denote something of the client's internal experience. There is much to be discerned by looking more closely at the look.

CHAPTER EIGHT

The significance of fame

In 1992 I was asked to give the Frank Lake Memorial Lecture, and I chose Fame as my subject since to my audience Frank Lake was a famous person. Most of my present readers will not have heard of him, so it is right to recall that he was a psychiatrist who had worked with a missionary society in India before returning to Britain and founding the Clinical Theology movement, which, in the 1960s and 1970s, especially trained a large number of clergy in pastoral counselling. I had edited one of his books (*Tight Corners in Pastoral Counselling*) and knew him from our joint membership of the *Contact* Editorial Board. The lecture gave me an opportunity to explore the subject, and later led to taking part in a research project with the late Petrushka Clarkson, who interviewed a number of relatively well-known therapists to ascertain what influence their "fame" had on their work with clients. Thus, the subject turned back on me, although I had not seen myself that way when working on the lecture.

* * *

"Some are born great, some achieve greatness,
and some have greatness thrust upon 'em . . ."

(*Twelfth Night*, 2. 5)

The year 1992 saw the five hundredth anniversary of Columbus's discovery of the New World. Spengemann wrote that year:

> The image of Columbus the man has changed apace over the years. In his lifetime, he was to some a tiresome upstart who had stumbled upon a few islands of dubious value, to others a valuable servant of the crown who had found a sea-route to Asia, and to himself a re-incarnated Isaiah and St John to whom God had shown the place where the world began and would end. A century later, he was seen as the visionary discoverer of a Spanish New World larger than Spain itself. By 1692, he had become an international figure who had opened the door to the western empires of England, France, and Holland. At the tricentennial, the "America" discovered by Columbus included the New World's first independent nation; and Columbus himself became a herald of democracy on both sides of the Atlantic. By 1892, there were more Spanish- and English-speakers in the New World than in the Old, and Columbus came to be seen by these Euro-Americans as the discoverer of themselves, a new people residing at the new centre of the world. And now that America has become the source of all the world's ills, the quincentennial Columbus is to repay Milton's debt to him by rehearsing *Paradise Lost* in the costume of Satan, the destroyer of the Garden and its stainless, vulnerable occupants. Successively a Cid, an Aeneas, a Moses, a Daniel Boone, and a Pandora, Columbus may be said quite literally to have grown with the country. [1992, pp. 5–6]

The perspective and distance of history enables us to see just how Columbus has become a screen upon whom particular cultural projections have been made. Such shifts in opinion help us to real-ize that even if we do not always see similar projections in our own society (and that, after all, is one of the functions of such a defence, that it is largely unconscious) they must also be present in relation to those who are currently prominent. Many of us have probably experienced the shift in projections that takes place even in the more limited time span of a generation. Politicians, in particular, take on a different perspective, especially in terms of mass opinion, depending on where and when they are viewed. They can be loved one moment, hated the next, scorned one year, and praised ten years later.

As a society, whether it is the larger political society that raises and topples the great, or the smaller societies and associations, we have images of our leaders. Sometimes we idealize them, some-times we denigrate them, and sometimes we even do this in fairly rapid succession. Recognition of the part we play, as members of society or of a particular society, in making people famous (or noto-rious) raises questions of whether those who are prominent in our society are really born great, whether it is they who achieve great-ness, or whether it might be that they have greatness thrust upon them. If it is true that "every country has the government it deserves" (de Maistre, 1851, p. 215), and, by implication, also that every group has the leadership it deserves, does fame tell us more about the group than about the leader?

In this chapter I examine the implications of this relationship between the famous and those who make them famous from a number of angles. First, I look at what, if anything, it is in the famous that predisposes them to seek, to adopt, or even reluctantly to accept, the position of fame for which we know them. Second, I ask what it is in those who follow or applaud that may attract them to the elevation of the famous, the leader, or the genius. Third, I examine the possibility of a dynamic between these first two areas of enquiry; fourth, ask if there are other factors that need to be taken into account, such as the spirit of an age or an idea in itself. I conclude by asking what any of this enquiry might have to tell us about the practice of psychotherapy and counselling.

The common assumption, in history and perhaps even in popu-lar thought, is that fame is a function of the famous, and not of the follower. The traditional way of trying to understand the famous is what Hollander calls "the trait approach to leadership" (1964, p. 4). In this approach, attempts are made to identify what personality traits distinguish "the great man". (This, sadly, is one place where the gender is specific, although we might indeed ask why not also "the great woman"?) In psychological studies, the idea of looking for individual traits has tended to be more attractive and relatively more accessible. That this is an over-simplification will become clear. Although fame is not to be equated solely with leadership, one description of leadership is "a relationship between a person exerting influence and those who are influenced . . . best seen within the framework of the group process" (ibid., p. 1).

If the famous really have "greatness thrust upon them" by the group, is there still something in them or about them that could lead us to say that they are "born great"? Is genius genetic? Or are they perhaps born into the right family of origin and first have "greatness thrust upon them" via the silver spoon? What personal characteristics might they have that help them to "achieve greatness" other than through learning or earning it?

According to one study of sixty-four eminent American scientists, including Nobel prize winners, the "average" eminent scientist is likely to be a higher than chance first-born child of a middle-class family, the son of a professional man, and either a sickly child or one who lost a parent at an early age. He is likely to have a very high IQ, to have done a great deal of reading in childhood, to have felt lonely and different, and to have been shy and aloof. He showed only a moderate interest in girls, married late, has two children, finds security in family life, and has a marriage more stable (and dull?) than average. Perhaps this is because he works very hard, often seven days a week and is completely satisfied with his vocation! He has few recreations, and avoids social, political, and religious life (Roe, 1952).

This psychological profile finds some confirmation from a discipline that few have heard of, known as "historiometry". This is the study of history through the application of the techniques of scientific research to historical and biographical records. One such historiometrist, Simonton, has studied what he calls the "laws of genius" (1984, p. vii). There is certainly some evidence for attributing some of the explanation of fame to nature and position of the family of origin. Simonton cites the work of the Goertzels (*ibid.*, p. 26f), who looked at the family influences on more than 400 twentieth century leaders and creative people. Birth order, for example, emerges as a variable that may partially explain how those who do achieve their fame. As in the study cited above, the first-born appear have a greater chance of success, although in the field of politics eminent people tend to be middle children, and only children are underrepresented among them (*ibid.*, p. 27). The frequency with which those who achieve fame have lost one or both parents in childhood or adolescence is significantly higher than the rest of the population, with the exception of two other groups: delinquents, and severely depressed and suicidal patients. Nevertheless, the incidence is not high enough to make this a principal contributor to fame. Other, perhaps more significant facts are socio-economic:

those who are prominent tend to come from upper-class families—a business or professional home. There are renowned families, too, where both inherited intelligence and the eminence of belonging to such a family are clearly factors. Attention has also been paid to the role model provided by a person's famous tutors or mentors. In this case, genius may partly be taught, but might also be modelled. Simonton concludes that "on the whole, environment seems to pay a much larger role than heredity in the emergence of genius" (*ibid.*, p. 41). Perhaps, more cynically, we might find the explanation for fame in what Merton calls "the Matthew effect" (1968), named after the passage "unto every one that hath shall be given, and he shall have abundance: but from him that hath not shall be taken away even that which he hath" (Matthew 25: 29). Those who have already begun to attract notice often get more favourable responses, and even more notice, than those who have so far attracted none.

What of factors within the person—that is, their personality and character? I have indicated that traditionally leaders have been thought to have distinguishable character traits that set them apart from their followers. Research into leadership qualities has not always taken into account that there are many different fields in which people achieve fame, and there might, therefore, be noticeable differences between the eminent in one field (say politics) and the renowned in another (say the arts). As a result of this failure to acknowledge different fields of fame, the results have often been disappointing. Intelligence, for example, does not seem a reliable predictor. There are many more highly intelligent people than there are those who achieve fame. In researching this topic, I have drawn upon the studies of different personality types and vocations, and I have woven them together in the hope that aspects from one field (for example, the charismatic leader) might throw some light upon another (for instance, that of the solitary artist). But I recognize the distinctions, too, and the fact that such cross-fertilization of personality characteristics and history does not always apply.

Perhaps motivation is one of those common factors. The need for achievement and the strong wish to achieve excellence seem to be important. The desire for power has also been examined: politicians with a strong need for achievement and power tend to be strong, although this could also be a dubious quality, since they are also the most likely to lead a country into war. It is possible, too, that emotional instability, or, more crudely, "madness", is another of those more common factors: as John Dryden wrote (1985),

> Great wits are sure to madness near allied,
> And thin partitions do their bounds divide.
>
> [*Absalom and Achitophel*, pt. i, ll. 163–164]

There seems to be more prevalence of manic–depressive personalities among creative people than among political leaders, and this personality type is more common among artists than scientists. Prentky (1980) lists twenty-five gifted men who have been diagnosed as schizophrenic, twenty-seven (including Freud!) with non-psychotic psychiatric disorders, and twenty-nine with affective disorders. But it is also conceivable that some symptoms such as depression are the consequence rather than the cause of fame. Many eminent people have to face opposition, envy, and adverse responses from their colleagues or society. It may also be that fame isolates a person, although here again introversion might be one of the marks of the eminent creative genius, more so than in the political leader. Among the little gems of information that Simonton passes on in his historiometric study is that Cavendish, the discoverer of hydrogen, never spoke at all to a woman, and never said more than a handful of words to a man.

It needs to be said of historiometry that while it furnishes some interesting information about leaders and creative people, including such anecdotes, it as yet does not provide enough evidence to settle any of these questions about the particular character and qualities of the famous. What it perhaps does most effectively is to challenge some of the old ideas we have about the character of leadership and eminence, which, of course, might be particularly pertinent in a society where the public relations people, and, indeed, sometimes the leaders themselves, either actively encourage, or at least take few steps to deny, the myths that surround them.

What is it, though, that leads the followers to follow?

It was assumed by Weber, one of the first to examine the charismatic leader, that a group of disciples must be attracted by the force and magnetism of their leader—it is the leader's magnetism that is important, and not the followers themselves. The only significance of those who accord fame is that you need others to identify those who become eminent. They are, as it were, only the backcloth that throws someone famous into relief—indeed such people "stand out from the crowd".

Freud suggested that the father-figure in an individual's childhood is the prototype of the "great man" (1939a, p. 555). Linked very closely with this assumption was Freud's adoption of the hypothesis of the "primal horde", a troop of equal companions led by an individual of superior strength, the primal father (1921c, p. 122ff). It is not clear whether Freud was suggesting an actual figure and actual horde, or whether he is adopting a metaphorical, mythical style in such references. It is difficult to accept that the highly rational and sceptical Freud could have believed in the actual existence of a primal father, except as a symbol to use in the understanding of groups and leadership. He proposed that the members of a group

> stand in need of the illusion that they are equally and justly loved by their leader, but the leader himself need love no one else, he may be of a masterful nature, absolutely narcissistic, self-confident and independent. [*ibid.*, p. 123]

Freud goes on to say that in an army or in a Church there exists this same "contrivance . . . the illusion that the leader loves all of the individuals equally and justly. This is simply an idealistic remodelling . . . of the primal horde". However, he also writes that in the primal horde the sons feel equally persecuted by the father (*ibid.*, p. 124). This other side of idealization—the persecutory—is an important aspect of this study of fame, to which I return below.

There is an alternative to Freud's symbol of the father–leader, a paternalistic picture that might be the product of the patriarchal society in which Freud lived. I have indicated already that the famous are mostly men. We have not yet have achieved much gender balance in positions of leadership, and we are still slow to recognize the contribution of those women who might just as equally have achieved fame in the arts, sciences, or the community in a less patriarchal system. That we might well need to revise the patriarchal explanation of leadership as essentially male is suggested by one analyst, whose study of charismatic leadership I draw upon below. Schiffer puts forward the idea of the "*primal mother* as the group pivot" (1973, p. 103, original italics). Surrogate mothers can be either sex. He suggests that allegiance to a leader might be traced back to the need for a mother who will look after us. There is more to it than this, because in the group itself, united by its allegiance to its leader and to her or his ideas, there is to some degree a realization of the wish for a return to the primitive unitary state of mother and baby—one for all and all for one. Indeed, given the darker side of symbiosis, the threat to loss of individuality, it is understandable that it is men who are elevated, or need to elevate themselves to eminent positions of apparent independence. Women are feared as being too powerful. As Schiffer sums it up,

> from the sum total of all the egocentric fantasies of the earliest offspring of primitive times, from such children with a common bond (necessary severance from the primal mother), evolves a collective narcissism, an egocentric self-commiseration society if you will, whose group pride continues even to this day to inspire the communal myth of mankind. In my supposition, group psychology has its first beginnings in the nursery. [1973, p. 105]

There is backing for this view in Kohut's self-psychology, delightfully explained by Josephine Klein in *Our Need for Others and Its Roots in Infancy* (1987). She explains Kohut's theory that in order to feel self-esteem a child needs to be have the experience of "feeling grand" in early infancy. But, where there might have been a failure in the environment to provide sufficient grounds for the phantasy of feeling grand, there is a secondary way of finding self-esteem through choosing (and to some extent even creating)

> a grand figure to identify with, which takes notice of the child and allows it to come close, and belong to the grandeur which this grand person possesses ... The child reaches out to explore and experiment and imitate. "I've just discovered that the world is full of a million wonderful things and THIS PERSON can make them happen and embodies them! Can I come close to that? Can I be like that?" [*ibid.*, pp. 218–219]

This environmental failure is likely to happen frequently in some societies; but in any case Klein makes it clear that everyone needs this secondary type of experience as well an early sense of well-being. It is also interesting to note how she draws attention to Kohut's assumption that while it is normally the mother who provides the first type of experience of feeling grand, this secondary type of identification and idealization is often provided by the father (*ibid.*, p. 219), which confirms the fact (although not the right) of men tending to be those who are accorded fame.

I have been referring to this point to that category of the famous who are leaders of groups. Frequently they are politicians, whether in the state or the church, or in smaller communities. They might equally be military leaders or managers of commerce and industry. The weakness of adopting such leaders as illustrative of my argument is, of course, that fame, as I have recognized above, is not confined to such public leaders. Many of those to whom we regard as "famous" were never prominent in that way. They have no recognized group or community to "follow" them, unless we stretch the point uncomfortably to include an audience hearing a Beethoven symphony, or watching one of Shakespeare's plays, or a professional scientific society listening to a learned paper. The literature on group psychology does not provide the same assistance to us in the matter of asking what else it is, apart from their own genius, that makes the Beethovens, Shakespeares, and Einsteins of this world famous. Perhaps exploration of the dynamic between the famous and those regard them so may provide more clues.

In the argument made above it is clear that some of the characteristics of a person who achieves fame meet the needs of people *en masse* to have someone famous (or in Klein's terms, "grand") with whom to identify. The relationship of the famous and those who award fame is possibly closer than I have so far expressed. There might be an even greater symbiotic quality to the relationship between the two.

In a study of personality and interpersonal relations, Jennings identifies seven marks of leadership, common attributes that she finds in many leaders. Most of these are to do with the way the leader conducts relationships with those who follow. He or she is seen by the followers as improving their social milieu. He or she widens the field of participation by others; knows when to censure and when to praise—leaders are not always pleasant, but will fight for what they consider right. They do not inflict their own negative feelings of anxiety or depression on others; they are able instead to hold their own counsel, and they only confide personal worries to selected people. The last two marks are the ability to establish rapport quickly and effectively with a wide range of people, and a greater capacity than normal to identify with others (Jennings, 1942, pp. 203–204). What may distinguish political, community, and group leaders from those who achieve fame through intellectual or artistic leadership is that the latter, while similarly holding their own counsel, and often being isolated men or women, through their creations often share in a sublimated way their anxieties and depression, and through their work demonstrate a greater capacity than normal to help others identify with them.

There is some confirmation of Jennings' identification of the relationship between leaders and those who follow them in a speculative study by Schiffer, a Canadian psychoanalyst. He admits that behaviourists might label his material "as unfounded assumption or juvenile exercises in mythology" (1973, p. 5.'). It is, none the less, worth summarizing his argument, since there are times when I think, without anything more by way of evidence than "feeling it in my bones", that he might provide some valuable leads as to some of the characteristics of the leader—he particularly looks at the charismatic leader—that make such a person a figure of popular attraction. He helps us to approach the question of what it is that those who accord fame might be drawn towards in those whom they elevate to fame.

Schiffer suggests eight possible elements in the image of the charismatic leader: the more of these eight elements that are evident, the greater the charm of the public figure. One of his suggestions is that the character of the charismatic leader reflects and expresses aspects of the followers' own infantile experience. It is not simply that a leader or someone famous stands for mother or father, those figures who at one time are supremely important in a child's life. A charismatic person also carries the projections of the child in the adult. So, if I have understood his argument correctly, the person who achieves fame also stands for the child, and lives out the child's phantasy of being powerful and important, even though in reality the child lacks power. There is some support for Schiffer's suggestion that the charismatic leader represents aspects of ourselves in Bass's research, which shows that we esteem most those whom we regard as most similar to us in attitudes, interests, and abilities (1960, p. 287).

Not all of Schiffer's eight marks of the charismatic are convincing, so I concentrate upon those that are.

First, the charismatic leader is in some way a foreigner. Schiffer gives examples of the German student Cohn-Bendit as leader of the Paris student uprising in 1968, of T. E. Lawrence as leader of the Arabs in Palestine in the First World War, of the Corsican Bonaparte as the leader of France, or the Austrian Hitler as the leader of Germany. He cites the Catholic Kennedy as charismatic leader of a predominantly Protestant country (1973, pp. 24–29). If Schiffer is right, what is it about the foreignness of a leader that makes this quality so attractive? Perhaps it is that such a person rises above familial envy and sibling rivalry.

But such envy and rivalry is just as present in his own country, making him unacceptable there. It is also relevant that one of the least attractive features of charismatic leadership is the leader who leads a savage, persecutory attack on those who do not belong, those who are in some way strangers and foreigners in the community. Perhaps the opposite of idealization is not just denigration, but also scapegoating, another form of projection. What makes charismatic leadership particularly dangerous is that it combines these two forces of projection in a potentially powerful, and, often in history, an actually destructive, cocktail. The leader who receives the idealized projections of the good object can incite the followers to project the bad parts of themselves on to an external object, and the idealized outsider then whips up their hatred against the denigrated outsider.

There are many examples of this, particularly in those who have preached anti-Semitism. There is, as I suggested in the opening paragraphs, where I drew attention to the swiftly changing fortunes of the famous, a very fine line that is easily crossed between *in extremis* idealization and persecution. Similarly, that fine line is seen in this characteristic in the way a charismatic leader often holds on to idealization through persecuting other foreigners. The leader could so easily be the one who should be attacked—and in the course of time probably will be. We also see here, in the first of Schiffer's elements of charismatic leadership, the symbiotic relationship that I look at more closely below, between the needs of the stranger who achieves fame to be accepted, and the needs of those who accord fame to avoid intra-familial rivalry, and the projection of their own wish as children to be accepted in what is to them still a foreign adult world.

Another of Schiffer's characteristics that I find convincing is his description of the charismatic as a hoaxer. There is a significant element of make-believe, and play-acting about the charismatic figure. He or she is able to adopt a *persona*, skilfully masking the private personality. Schiffer, rather appropriately, uses an oral image here for the way in which the public can become "a sucker" for the images that the charismatic leader creates. At the same time we know that we are being hoaxed, that it is an act, and yet we admire the ability of the charismatic figure to get away with it (1973, p. 51): as children, there must have been many times we wished we could pull such a fast one on our parents. So, the illusions in some sense deceive us, but they also tell us something about our own similar inner child's wish to deceive. The first quality, that of the stranger or the foreigner, also helps to preserve the illusion that is part of the charismatic appeal. In the political climate of today, we might even call it "spin".

Schiffer neglects a much more positive quality to such an illusion, which Winnicott provides in his idea of the mother creating an illusion for her baby through a transitional object. Mother, in a sense, hoaxes the baby, although Winnicott does not put it in that way. When functioning as a group therapist, I similarly have sensed this quality of creating an illusion, so that as the therapist I am seen at different times by different people in different ways, sometimes even standing for the group itself. What has been clear in some groups is that the group members do not wish to meet me outside in other settings, because this would shatter their illusion, an illusion that they have helped to create, which they are able to play with in order to carry out their therapeutic task. There is, thus, a co-operative venture between the therapist and the members of a group: a type of suspension of reality, a type of hoax if you will, which everyone is aware of and yet values as therapeutic.

A third characteristic is that the leader often has some mark of imperfection, "a subtle stigma" (Schiffer, 1973, p. 54). Here we can point to the lameness of Jacob, the swollen foot of Oedipus, the diminutive Napoleon, Churchill's lisp, or perhaps the slight failings of the leader which make them more endearing—although it is not clear why, for instance, some politicians seem to acquire more attraction through falling short morally while others are destroyed by their mistakes. The idea that the leader or genius can fail is sometimes a feature of their attractiveness. Schiffer points out that in some ancient near eastern rituals, kings were emasculated, so that they were no longer perfect. He suggests that, strong though our wish is for a perfect object, we are also attracted to someone who has a slight imperfection, since it strengthens the phantasy that their position is also obtainable by us, despite the imperfections that we are conscious of in ourselves.

Schiffer, like Weber in his study of the charismatic leader, identifies the importance of a sense of calling, and points out the often religious or quasi-religious aura of the leader, although he links this with the promise of a specific idea or set of ideas: charismatic leadership consists of more than a magical aura or a particular personality trait. We might observe, in linking leadership with examples of genius in other spheres of endeavour, that others whom we now see as famous did not simply promise, but actually delivered ideas, in words, in art, and in music that certainly have a quasi-religious, if not indeed a religious, appeal. Schiffer also notes, as Weber did in identifying the ascetic quality of the leader, that the leader is often turned in on himself, cut off from others and self-reliant in a narcissistic way. The psycho-historian Weinstein suggests that the creative and intellectual endeavour requires a person to possess a degree of narcissism. The intellectual has to believe in her- or himself (1980). Perhaps there is a balance to their narcissism in the motivating force in many a genius or leader from an idea or set of ideas: this suggests to their followers, who see them as god-like, that they, too (the leaders), have allegiance to a higher plane.

Some of the other marks of the charismatic leader in Schiffer's study have already been referred to in Jennings' study of leadership (the willingness to fight for beliefs, and what Schiffer calls "lifestyle innovation" [1973, p. 54]), or have been alluded to above (such as social position). There is one other characteristic that Schiffer identifies, that of sexual mystique, which he accurately portrays not as being one of sexual prowess (which some authors [e.g., Cell, 1974] have suggested is an indicator of charismatic leadership), but as being surrounded by ambiguity. It is not that the famous show no sign of sexuality, but that it is not blatant.

Such sexuality is subtle. It is hidden and a mystery, but it is there none the less, and it represents an attractive force. As Schiffer states,

"The appeal of the strip-teaser rests not with her nudity but with her G-string. It is in the no-man's land between what is exposed and what is hidden that the story of charismatic sexuality takes place" (1973, p. 48). Indeed, exposure of actual sexuality can lead to rapid deflation of the charismatic image. The leader, like our parents, must in some way obviously be a sexual being, but at the same time must not flout it. The earliest matrix for sexual charisma, suggests Schiffer, is the primal scene: that is, parental intercourse.

What Schiffer suggestively observes is that the appeal of the charismatic leader is as much his sexual diffidence as his sexual prowess (*ibid.*, p. 46). Such a feature reflects the ambivalence of childhood phantasies and wishes: alternate feelings of wanting to be big but also feeling very small. The leader reminds us of ourselves, and appears at least to be at ease with all that, to be successful despite and because of it.

Sexuality is not given as much attention in studies of leadership or genius as it might be. Brown, for example, only briefly addresses it when he writes, "Two factors of a semi-biological nature are important in leadership, intelligence and psychosexual appeal. Of these, probably the most important is intelligence" (1936, p. 347). Freud endows sexual and oedipal significance to the primal horde and to the leading father-figure, who occupies such a position in many other species than the human as a result of his physical strength and (by implication) his sexual prowess. But he also makes clear in respect of artists that in them is perhaps the finest form of sexual sublimation, since the artist "allows his erotic and ambitious wishes full play in the life of phantasy" but comes back to reality "making use of his special gifts to mould his phantasies into truths of a new kind, which are valued . . . as precious reflections of reality" (1911b, p. 137).

In these descriptions of the characteristics of leaders, I have wished to examine the close relationship between the famous and those who follow them. While earlier I drew upon Freud's theory of group psychology involving projection of the ego-ideal by group members on to the leader, it is Bion's somewhat different theory that helps us more in identifying the mutual relationship between leader and group, because Bion uses the concept not of projection, but of projective identification. In projection, the person upon whom the projection is made is not psychologically changed by the process: the projected figure remains in the eye of the beholder. In projective identification, the person takes on the projection and actually becomes more like the projected figure. (This is most clearly seen in intimate and marital relationships.) In distinguishing his own theory of group dynamics from Freud, Bion states that Freud views identification as almost entirely a process of introjection by the ego. The crowd or the group gives up its own ego to the leader, and in return models itself on the ego-ideal that it sees in the leader. Bion, on the other hand, recognizes that "the leader is as much the creature of the basic assumption as any other member of the group" (1961, p. 177), basing this not on introjection alone, but on a simultaneous process of projective identification. So, the leader is not simply someone who creates a group that adheres to his ideas, but is also another individual who is moulded by the requirements of the group. "The 'loss of individual distinctiveness' applies to the leader of the group as much as anyone else—a fact that probably accounts for some of the posturing to which leading figures are prone" (*ibid.*). Bion suggests that one of the qualities of the leader is the capacity for rapid identification with any other member of the group; he is, if you like, a chameleon-like figure who can take on the colour, the stereotypes, and the projections of those who happen to be closest at the time. Bion thus confirms the value of many of Jennings' and Schiffer's descriptions of the charismatic leader. (The "he" here needs to be noted. Is it the same with a woman leader? Or does the co-operative style of many women's groups suggest a different dynamic? This question is much less addressed, if at all, by these [largely male] authors.)

Redl's work suggest that it is not so much a personality *trait* as a particular personality *attribute* that leaders need, which he calls "group psychological flexibility". The leader is able to respond to and to issue different stimuli in varying situations, and to a diversity of individuals as well. Redl (1942) lists ten types of person who are central to the groups, reinforcing or bringing about group integration: the patriarchal sovereign, the leader, the tyrant, the love object, the object of aggression, the organizer, the seducer, the hero, the bad influence, and the good example. Perhaps this is as good a list as any of those who achieve fame in different spheres of action, enabling fame (which I have suggested throughout is on a razor edge) to include infamy as well!

In his philosophy, Plato supposed that in sensing and experiencing we temporarily partake in or communicate with a higher Form or Idea. When something is beautiful it partakes of the Form or Idea of Beauty. In psychoanalytic language we can describe the breast as an ideal object, but Winnicott introduces a somewhat different concept that has something of this Platonic quality. He suggests that a baby, in its need to be fed, has already created an "idea" of the breast before mother offers the actual breast; the actual breast is, in some way, a temporary partaking of the ideal breast (1988, pp. 100–102). And, although we know that it is mother who allows the baby the illusion of having created the breast, there is a sense, he goes on to say, in which the baby truly is creative, as long as the mother is responsive enough to make the creative thought become real through offering the breast at the right time. Phantasy does not simply follow experience: the ideal breast does not simply follow the experience of the breast. Winnicott also wonders whether there might not be a primary creativity, which is, as it were *ex nihilo*—we can produce without having first taken in (*ibid.*, p. 110). Phantasy creates a type of Ideal, of which experience then may partake. It may be appropriate also to suggest that in this matter of fame, which includes people who are extraordinarily creative, that it is not only that we accord them fame for what they have given us, but because they make real what is already present in us. As Schiffer writes, "All leaders . . . are to a meaningful degree creations of the people" (1973, p. 6).

If, therefore, a famous person is in some way a vehicle or a vessel for the creation of ideas, whether in political, intellectual, or artistic form, it is a relatively simple step to consider whether fame might also not be a by-product of historical and social accidents. Freud noted this in contrasting the type of history writing that is about the worship of heroes and

the modern tendency . . . towards tracing back the events of human history to more concealed, general and impersonal factors, to the compelling influence of economic conditions, to alterations in food habits, to advances in the use of materials and tools . . . Individuals have no other part to play in this than as exponents or representatives of group trends, which are bound to find expression and do so in these particular individuals largely by chance. [1939a, p. 106]

Freud dismissed this latter view, but it finds expression in the historiometric study of the relationship between the individual and what has been called "the spirit of the age", or *zeitgeist*. Hegel described how "the great man of his age is the one who can put into words the will of his age, tell his age what its will is and accomplish it" (Simonton, 1984, pp. 134–135). Although Simonton finds mixed statistical evidence for certain themes that may link a particular *zeitgeist* to particular types of genius, his conclusion is finely stated:

> "Being the right person" is almost as important as "being in the right place at the right time" . . . A certain type of genius may have a higher probability of accomplishment when the spirit of the times takes one form, whereas another type of genius may have an advantage when the zeitgeist shifts to another emphasis. [*ibid.*, p. 165]

There is some research that shows the possibility of an interaction between political *zeitgeist* and birth order. An only child is more likely to become a leader when civil conflict breaks out, a first-born child during times of international crisis and warfare, a middle-born child when a nation is at peace, and a last-born when revolution is the spirit of the times. Far-fetched though such research seems, it suggests there may some truth in there being a right person for the right time, and that historical accident may be an important factor in the rise to fame. Prentky provides examples of periods of history where "the spirit of the age" seems to have given birth to an extraordinarily large number of eminent and creative people—the Age of Pericles in Athens in the fifth century BC; the one hundred year period in the advance of science from Bacon through to Halley, which might be called the Age of Newton; the Renaissance for art, sculpture, and architecture; or the fifty-year span from 1870 to 1920 that witnessed the births of twenty-seven major scientists, twenty-two of whom have received a Nobel prize (1980, pp. 183–184).

I doubt whether the source of fame lies simply in the individual genius, and so find it difficult to accept that the individual alone is responsible for what he or she creates. Although the creations of musicians, artists, and men and women of literature certainly stand on their own, a present day critical approach seeks to understand both the creator and also the created, by reference to each other and to their historical and cultural context. We learn more when we study the dynamic relationship between the famous, the age and the time in which they live, what they produce or create or stand for that brings them fame, and those who honour them.

It is time to descend from the realms of research and abstract thought, and ask what lessons therapists and counsellors might take from these ideas. One of the aims of psychoanalysis, which influences psychodynamic therapists in particular, is to help eliminate the excessive influence of the unconscious, first on daily life, and second on the capacity to reason, and to help people understand their emotional experiences and patterns of relationships. Therapists, therefore, need to be critical of the way in which adults continue to idealize others, including political or cultural leaders. Idealization of others tends towards infantilization of oneself. Unfortunately, psychoanalysis and other forms of therapeutic enterprise too often demonstrate a similar idealization of their own teachers and leaders, failing to interpret sufficiently strongly the transference phenomena that they see so clearly (and sometimes too reductively) everywhere else. The first lesson might, therefore, be one of caution about according anyone fame, and about the consequences of such idealization.

Second, if it is true that those who achieve fame carry much for other people, it is necessary to consider the effects that this has on the famous. As Bion describes it, the leader can be someone "whose qualification for the job is that his personality has been obliterated, an automaton, 'an individual who has lost his distinctiveness'" (1961, p. 178). He goes on to suggest that this is not only a possible recipe for disaster for the group, but a personal disaster for the leader, whose individuality is squeezed out of existence and becomes devoid of substance. Anyone who has experienced being drained, or wrung out, has had a taste of that experience, which is often defended in public figures by the persona that they erect around themselves—a persona that works only as long as people feed into it. Similarly, part of our concern should be lest the innovator and the famous become a "possession" of those who idolize them, trying to feed off them more and more. In the end, they are in danger of entering a vicious circle of having to go on being original in order to provide and earn new occasions for praise. As a society, we need to allow the eminent to be ordinary, uncreative, and un-everything-we-want-of-them, so that they can find space for themselves and for being creative in their own time.

These implications suggest the need to lessen the amount of idealization process, which has a tendency in the end to reduce rather than support those who achieve greatness, as well as diminish those who thrust it upon them. Studies of what makes for greatness suggest that there exists a far greater potentiality for greatness than the now disputed theory of "traits" of greatness allowed. How might therapists and counsellors help create a climate as well as foster the potentiality for their clients to become creative and "famous" (i.e., respected, as well as achieving self-respect, whether in the smaller or larger arena) themselves?

There are many thoughtful, intelligent, creative, and inspired people who never achieve fame and eminence in terms of public recognition. Creativity and innovation do not always have to be original to give a person a sense of having discovered something for themselves and, in doing so, to have achieved a sense of themselves as unique and independent. Therapy provides an arena, normally with an audience of only one, of course, in which people may express themselves and discover themselves in ways which are as important to them as the expression and discoveries of the famous have become important for the wider culture and society. One of the features of individual therapy is that it treats each client as special. For an hour a week the client can be centre stage: it may be alarming at first to be in the limelight in this way. But, one hopes, therapy helps to ease the anxiety and self-censoriousness at having such special attention, and nurtures instead the specialness that should, of course, be the birthright of every child. Therapy might help to realize what Schiffer identifies as "the hero (or heroine) . . . an intrinsic universal image of every individual at one or another stage in personal development" (1973, p. 7). Therapists can provide the encouragement to clients to express themselves, and can provide the support that will nurture their originality, so that they will not give up in the face of opposition, criticism, or inattention.

This is not reductionism, a type of dumbing-down to the lowest common factor, which destroys creativity and might result in mediocrity. It does not, to paraphrase W. S. Gilbert (*The Gondoliers*), seek to make everybody anybody, but anybody somebody.

In a book on leadership, Carlisle is quoted as calling great men "beginners", because they see further than others and desire things more strongly than others. His (and we must obviously read "her" here as well) activities are the conscious and free expression of the inevitable and unconscious natural course of things. But this "is not only for 'beginners', not only for 'great' men . . . It is open for all who have eyes to see, ears to hear and hearts to love their neighbours" (quoted in Gouldner, 1965). The passage concludes: "The concept great is a relative concept".

CHAPTER NINE

Have we lost fate?

H aving some years before delivered the lecture from which the previous chapter is taken, it was a surprise when I found myself honoured in a similar way, although it was quite clear this was not to be an annual memorial lecture since I was asked to deliver the first Michael Jacobs lecture myself at the University of Leicester in 2006! Nevertheless, it was a strange experience, and remains so when more distinguished people than myself deliver the lecture in subsequent years. Why did I choose Fate? Perhaps because, as I suggest in the previous chapter, any fame I might have achieved is only partly of my doing. Opportunities have come my way, Fate has played its hand; and although I might have taken those opportunities, nevertheless I would not have got anywhere without others opening doors that enabled me to find more of myself, and therefore have the privilege of following through my ideas in a more public arena than most people can. The subject also appealed because it enabled me to dig around in some of the earlier psychoanalytic literature, and to examine what others, similarly interested in the topic, had made of it. I seldom write anything new; I do, perhaps, bring the old to life.

* * *

Writing to his colleague Wilhelm Fliess on 15 October 1897, Freud penned words that were to become significant not only for psycho-analysis, but for Western culture:

> A single idea of general value dawned on me. I have found, in my own case too [the phenomenon of], being in love with the mother and jealous of my father, and now I now consider it a universal event in early childhood . . . If this is so, we can understand the gripping power of *Oedipus Rex*, in spite of all the objections that reason raises against the presupposition of fate . . . the Greek legend seizes upon a compulsion which everyone recognizes because he senses its existence within himself. Everyone in the audience was once a budding Oedipus in fantasy, and each recoils in horror from the dream fulfilment here transplanted into reality, with the full quantity of repression which separates his infantile state from his present one. [Masson, 1985, p. 272]

In time, the term "Oedipus complex" was the name given to this "single idea" and the theory became one of the foundation stones of psychoanalysis (Freud, 1923a, p. 247). But the Oedipus myth con-tains, of course, another factor, one which Freud passes over when he writes of the power of *Oedipus Rex*. While not ignoring fate, or rather the Fates, Freud is more interested in what fate dictates for Oedipus, than in the role of fate in the myth and in the play. The point is this, and it is one which to some extent must vex anyone who embraces the Oedipus complex: Oedipus actually tried to avoid parricide and incest, because he knew that was what the oracle predicted for him, but he could not, whether in action or later by his denial of the truth that stared him in the face, escape his fate. That makes it harder on Oedipus than, for instance, the conse-quences of their own action or inaction make it hard for Othello, Lear, Hamlet, or Macbeth.

Yet, Freud does not elsewhere neglect the Fates. Two notable references to the Fates appear in *The Interpretation of Dreams* and in his essay "The theme of the three caskets" (1913f, pp. 289–301). But, in both instances, what Freud does is to demythologize the Fates and turn them into symbols that more obviously fit his associations. So, from his dream, which we know (Anzieu, 1986, p. 384) occurred in October or November 1898, Freud associates first to three women who appear in the first novel he ever read, which then leads him to think of the three Fates in Greek mythology who spin the destiny of men and women, and then of the mother who gives life and the first nourishment to the baby. The Fates are thus subsumed ultimately in the figure of mother. They receive rather more attention in his short essay "The theme of the three caskets". The three caskets to which he refers in that 1913 essay are used by Portia in *The Merchant of Venice* as a test for various suitors. They are made of gold, silver, and lead, respectively, and if a suitor chooses the right casket, the one that contains a key, he wins her hand in marriage. What interested Freud was the significance of *choosing*, as well as the significance of the *lead* casket, because it is in fact the one of least value that yields the prize. He observes that the casket itself is a symbol of what is essential in a woman, that she, too, is a container, and he takes three other examples of choice. The first is the contest at the start of *King Lear* where the old abdicating king asks each of his three daughters, Goneril, Regan, and Cordelia, to declare how much they love him. The second is that of Cinderella—again one of three daughters; Cinderella is the one of least value, but it is she who wins the Prince. And the third story that Freud draws upon is that of the Judgement of Paris, the shepherd who has to choose between three goddesses which is the fairest, the winner receiving a golden apple. He, too, declares the *third* one presented to him as the most beautiful.

But, Freud writes, it is not just beauty that is one of the qualities of each of the "third" women—Cordelia loves and yet is silent; Cinderella hides, and we might equate hiddenness and silence. Bassanio declares that the plainness or the paleness of the lead moves him more than eloquence—silence is perhaps being referred to again there. And, in Offenbach's libretto of the Judgement of Paris, the third goddess, Aphrodite, is silent. Freud draws the conclusion that silence equates with death, and finally he suggests how these sets of three, whether caskets or women, and particularly the three goddesses in the myth of the Judgement of Paris, are paralleled by the three Fates in Greek mythology, the third of whom represents death.

The three Fates, known as the Moirae, are three sister-goddesses, although Freud says they developed out of a single figure who personified inevitable fate. The first, Clotho, spins the thread of life and represents birth, although Freud's description of her is that she represents "the innate disposition with its fateful implications" (1913f, p. 298). The second, Lachesis, "seems", in Freud's citation, "to denote 'the accidental that is included in the regularity of destiny'" (*ibid.*, p. 298); or, as others have expressed it, "the thread of life itself". The third sister-goddess, Atropos, is the one who cuts the thread of life, and represents the inevitable, death, or a state of never changing, from which we get the word "atrophy". But, as in his association to the Fates following his dream in 1898, Freud shifts the emphasis back to the human, and he concludes his essay with these words:

> We might argue that what is represented here are the three inevitable relations that a man has with a woman: the woman who bears him, the woman who is his mate and the woman who destroys him; or that they are the three forms taken by the figure of the mother in the course of a man's life—the mother herself, the beloved one who is chosen after her pattern, and lastly the Mother earth who receives him once more. But [and here he refers to King Lear], it is in vain that an old man yearns for the love of a woman as he had it first from his mother; the third of the Fates alone, the silent Goddess of Death, will take him into her arms. [*ibid.*, p. 301]

Freud certainly does not himself avoid the theme of death: indeed, a year after he wrote that essay the outbreak of the Great War brought home to him the need to grapple with the psychological problem of death. But this essay on the three caskets, as with some of his other speculative essays, uses arguments that are somewhat tortuous, that are more associations than logical steps. He asserts that what we most want to avoid is death, and that we have turned the third of the Fates, who might be called the goddess of death, into the goddess of love, Aphrodite, whom Paris chooses as the most beautiful. We avoid the theme of death and concentrate more, in these different stories that he examines, on love. Freud observes that in many myths the great Mother-goddesses are both creators and destroyers—goddesses of life and of death. Although choice is a part of all these stories, there is no choice about death—it is an inevitable part of our destiny. The stories, therefore, defend us against both the inevitability of, and the fact of, death.

Yet, his closing words in the essay show how Freud yet again slips away from the Fates, and relates them as much to the relationships of a man with women, including the mother. While not avoiding the fact of death, his exposition loses the force of the Fates generally. Perhaps that is what might be expected of one who drew upon mythology more as symbolizing unconscious forces, and who essentially in the end rationalizes those symbols. What is lost, then, is a different set of forces, the forces of fate, which, for example, impel Oedipus to act out the prophecy that he would kill his father and marry his mother. He, and indeed Laius and Jocasta, his true parents, do everything they can to avoid the path of fate, his parents resorting to what they believe to be infanticide. Oedipus puts as great a distance as he can between himself and those he thought were his parents, Polybus and Merope. But none of them can escape: fate dictates that he should meet his father, not knowing him to be his father, at the crossroads, and Oedipus kills him in the heat of a quarrel; that he should find his way to Thebes and marry his mother, not knowing her to be that. He cannot avoid fate. That aspect is not drawn out at all by Freud.

This inevitability is not confined to the story of Oedipus. It is a theme that appears in the fairy story of Sleeping Beauty. At the christening of the infant princess, the thirteenth fairy, who has been left uninvited to the celebrations, curses the child, saying that she will prick her finger upon a spindle and die. Another fairy changes the curse of death to sleep, but this does not stop the king from ordering that all the spindles in the palace must be destroyed; indeed, that all the spindles in the kingdom must be destroyed. Such desperate measures prove of no avail, because the child, now entering adolescence, explores a part of the royal palace that escaped the king's attention, finds an old woman spinning flax, and pricks her finger on the spindle. There is no escaping Fate.

Following Freud, mainstream psychoanalysis has largely given the significance of Fate scant attention. There is a major exception in Lacan. In his seminar 11, *The Four Fundamental Concepts of Psychoanalysis* (1977), Lacan formulates a theory of fate in relation to trauma and neurosis. It is beyond the scope of this chapter and author to integrate Lacan into the ideas expressed here, but the difference between the Real (chance or fate) and the Symbolic none the less has relevance. A more obviously relevant exception is Helene Deutsch's paper, published in 1930, entitled "Hysterical fate neurosis". I draw here briefly on an article by Donald Kaplan (1984) for an account of that paper. Kaplan comments that

> the idea of a psychopathology of fate or what had come to be called a fate neurosis has failed to retain any established place in the structure of psychoanalytic thought. The clinical observations and theoretical formulations, to which the idea of a fate neurosis answered, have been subsumed in the course of things by more fundamental and systematic conceptualizations. [*ibid.*, p. 240]

Nevertheless, Kaplan calls Deutsch's paper "an unread classic . . . a classic in the sense that its sustained consideration of a particular subject achieved an originality that has not been superseded" (*ibid.*, pp. 241, 240). Furthermore, as he writes, it is often useful to revisit an idea that has not been taken up.

Deutsch presents a case in her paper to "illustrate the typical features of a 'fate neurosis'" (Deutsch, 1930[1965], p. 17), which can be summarized as follows: a young woman who was intellectually gifted entered one relationship where her intellectual gifts were played down, followed by a second relationship with an older man where she felt very fulfilled. This man secured a divorce and they were going to get married. But, just when everything seemed to be working out for the good, he was called away to his ex-wife's sickbed, something that apparently presented no problem to her; but she then had a disastrous fling with a young man for whom she felt nothing, got pregnant, had an abortion and attempted suicide. Kaplan links the case to Freud's examination of people who have achieved the very satisfaction they were seeking, and yet then fall ill (1916d).

These cases may not at first sight have much to do with fate, and we may wonder what the term "fate neurosis" means. Kaplan summarizes the issue:

> By the time she presented herself to Dr Deutsch, the emotionality of the suicide attempt and the events that led up to it had subsided, and in her first interview she appeared calm, self-possessed, and at a loss to say what she needed treatment for. As the interview drew on she [Deutsch] began to detect something vaguely morbid in the larger story she told of her life but nothing so definite or acute as to account for the crisis she had recently brought about. And so the analysis began with this puzzling contradiction.

Although the patient's attempt at suicide was a culmination of a succession of events in her love life, all that she could repeat about it was that it occurred in the midst of preparations to marry a man she regarded with great respect and with whom she felt fulfilled, amorous, high spirited. [1984, 244–245]

Unfortunately, this case takes us little further, except in as much as this patient, and those described by Freud in his essay on character types (1916d), suggest that it is life circumstances that lead to some sort of breakdown, not through the inhibition of impulses as would be expected in the usual formation of neurosis. There also seems to be something about character here as well, which is relevant to Fate: that while there may well be reasons why particular characteristics develop in any one person, the ensuing character is something which that person carries through life in a fateful way, with little that ever alters the fundamental character. In Deutsch's patient, for example, there appeared to be

a clear and long-standing complaint about her life. In an otherwise subjectively uneventful childhood and adolescence, she was increasingly troubled by the fact that vague inner difficulties prevented her from fulfilling her intellectual ambitions to enter a university and pursue a profession. [1984, p. 246]

Or, to put it another way, in the reply that Freud gave to the fictitious questioner who objects, "You yourself tell me that what I am suffering from is probably connected with my circumstances and fate. You can't change anything about that. So how are you going to help me?", Freud replies,

I do not doubt that it would be easier for fate to take away your suffering than it would for me. But you will see for yourself that much has been gained if we succeed in turning your hysterical misery into common unhappiness. Having restored your inner life, you will be better able to arm yourself against that unhappiness. [Freud, 1895d, p. 305]

Without going any further into Deutsch's case history, or indeed pursuing her particular line on fate, it is worth noting that there are, of course, many of the usual explanations as to why her patient attempted suicide, and why she was drawn into the particular relationships she describes. Kaplan rightly criticizes the case, for Deutsch's "exclusive emphasis . . . on her patient's reconciliations with personal destiny, portrayed largely in terms of active attainments"; and for the way Deutsch "obscures considerations of the patient's intrapsychic experiences and processes, modifications of which also figure in the goals and outcomes of analysis. In this and other things she makes too little of too much" (Kaplan, 1984, p. 260). Nevertheless, what Deutsch does is to stress the significance of external events as much as the relevance of long developed character, and that these broader issues have as much significance as what we might now be called "precipitating circumstances".

This excursion into a cul-de-sac of psychoanalytic intellectual history merely highlights the absence of any sustained thought about fate itself. Analytic thought prefers to concentrate upon the inner world, and pays less attention to the force of external circumstances as contributors to our mental state in their own right. Existentialism fares better, and no doubt is more clearly stated in the theory of existential therapy than it usually is in psychodynamic or psychoanalytic therapy. Nevertheless, there are hints of it in mainstream analytic theory. Freud's description of each of the three Fates provides some useful leads.

The first of the Fates is Clotho, the sister who spins the thread of life and represents birth. Here Freud's description of her, that she represents "the innate disposition with its fateful implications" (1913f, p. 298) is particularly apt.

Fate deals us a hand at our conception, at our birth, and in the crucial early months and years of infancy. Ian McEwan, in his novel *Saturday* (2005), puts it this way

> It's a commonplace of parenting and modern genetics that parents have little or no influence on the characters of their children. You never know who you are going to get. Opportunities, health, prospects, accent, table manners—these might lie within your power to shape. But what really determines the sort of person who's coming to live with you is which sperm finds which egg, how the cards in two packs are chosen, then how they are shuffled, halved and spliced at the moment of recombination. Cheerful or neurotic, kind or greedy, curious or dull, expansive or shy and anywhere in between; it can be quite an affront to parental self-regard, just how much of the work has already been done. On the other hand, it can let you off the hook. [2005, p. 25]

Towards the end of the book the central character, the neuro-surgeon Henry Perowne, contemplates his assailant Baxter, whom Henry has seen is showing indications of Huntington's Disease:

> The door of his consciousness is beginning to close . . . This is his dim, fixed fate, to have one tiny slip, an error of repetition in the codes of his being, in his genotype, the modern variant of the soul, and he must unravel. [2005, p. 279]

McEwan is particularly concerned in that novel with the neuro-logical causes of mental disturbance, but the point is well made: that we are conceived and born with particular features, into fami-lies that live and relate in particular circumstances, and into a soci-ety that has its own particular values and issues. Helen Deutsch's patient's fate was that she was born a woman, and that she had a highly developed intellectual capacity, born into a society, more particularly at that time than now, where the intellectual woman was seen by many men as an uncomfortable figure. There are strengths and weaknesses in our physical make-up, some of which may be apparent in the early months of life, some of which show themselves much later, lying dormant over the years until a genetic disposition is revealed.

We live sometimes with knowledge of this innate disposition, sometimes without it until it comes to the surface. And, while it is, of course, possible through genetic engineering and other wonders of medicine and surgery to overcome some of these genetic faults, we are never free of them, and even when caught out by one of them and apparently cured, live with the threat of them still. Much of the time we are naturally in deliberate denial—life would be impossibly heavy if we constantly contemplated all our possible ills; but this particular fate, the innate disposition is with us always.

Psychoanalytic theory has, of course, followed Freud in recog-nizing the variables that influence psychological development, with Melanie Klein, for example, according a place to "constitutional disposition", and "the dual determination of development by con-stitution and environment" (1988, p. 420); or Anna Freud describ-ing how "child analysts have to remember that the detrimental external factors which crowd their view achieve their pathological significance by way of interaction with the innate disposition and acquired, internalized libidinal and ego attitudes" (1965, p. 51). It is easy, as therapists who wish to be able to influence outcome for good, either to assign too little significance to innate disposition or to fail to recognize how much innate disposition weighs upon the patient, since the burden of their perceived or actual weakness is something they live with every day.

The second of the Fates is the figure of Lachesis, who, in the quotation cited by Freud, "seems to denote 'the accidental that is included in the regularity of destiny'" (1913f, p. 298). Whereas the Fate sister Clotho takes us in the direction of determinism, in as much as innate disposition, external factors, and internal objects appear to determine a person's character, the accidental takes us more in the direction of fatalism; the difference between determinism and fatalism being, according to Bjerke, that determinism

> assumes a causal sequence of events ... it is the assumption of determinism that the causality of man's will—as everything else—is determined by that which went before, but not without influence on the events which follow. On the other hand, pure fatalism does not recognize the will as a contributory link in the course of events. [1995, p. 81]

It might, therefore, be possible to ameliorate or indeed alter what is determined, but this type of fate we cannot alter; we only build some defences against it in the hope that they will lessen the impact of the accidental.

Bollas (1989) makes another distinction that should be noted here, between fate and destiny. The two are not quite synonymous, destiny being a more positive force "a course that is a potential in one's life" (1989, p. 31). He posits a primary dynamic force in human development that he terms the "destiny drive", which seeks to use objects to express and develop the "true self". In contrast, there are those who are fated, leading to the development of a false self. Despite the obvious parallels to Carl Rogers's "actualising tendency", such a division seems to suggest those who suffer from fate cannot be true to themselves. Yet, it may be fate that is the making of a person's "true" character. And many will be familiar with the way external circumstances, whether accidental events or through another's actions, can either impede or provide opportunity for the fulfilment of one's destiny.

Random events, which can have such impact upon people's lives, are often called chance: "as chance would have it"; or luck: "just my luck"; or, indeed, fate: "I'm fated". Hardy's poem "The convergence of the twain" makes it appear to the poet that the Titanic's fate is determined, whereas an alternative view would be that this was pure chance, an accident that the designers of the ship attempted to defend against in building her to be unsinkable, but where chance dictated otherwise:

> In a solitude of the sea
> Deep from human vanity,
> And the Pride of Life that planned her, stilly couches she.
>
> Steel chambers, late the pyres
> Of her salamandrine fires,
> Cold currents thrid, and turn to rhythmic tidal lyres.
>
> Over the mirrors meant
> To glass the opulent
> The sea-worm crawls—grotesque, slimed, dumb, indifferent.
>
> Jewels in joy designed
> To ravish the sensuous mind
> Lie lightless, all their sparkles bleared and black and blind.
>
> Dim moon-eyed fishes near
> Gaze at the gilded gear
> And query: "What does this vaingloriousness down here?" . . .
>
> Well: while was fashioning
> The creature of cleaving wing,
> The Immanent Will that stirs and urges everything
>
> Prepared a sinister mate
> For her—so gaily great -
> A Shape of Ice, for the time far and dissociate.
>
> And as the smart ship grew
> In stature, grace and hue,
> In Shadowy silent distance grew the Iceberg too.
>
> Alien they seemed to be:
> No mortal eye could see
> The intimate welding of their later history,

Or sign that they were bent
By paths coincident
On being anon twin halves of one august event,

Till the Spinner of the Years
Said "Now!" And each one hears,
And consummation comes, and jars two hemispheres.

[1979, pp. 249–250]

We are surrounded by chance events, accidents that can seldom
be predicted. Even though some accidents are waiting to happen,
or the predisposition for them to happen is greater in some situations or some people's lives than in others, when and where they
will happen is chance. Accidents in nature are examples—the earthquake, the forest fire, the tsunami, or accidents of history, or trig-
gers that lead to an economic crash or the outbreak of a war. There
are parts of the environment where certain accidents of nature are
more likely to occur, such as the San Andreas fault, or swathes of
forest in hot and dry climates. Physical laws such as the
Guttenberg/Richter power law in relation to earthquakes might
state that each time you double the energy in the earthquake it
becomes four times as rare, but, as Mark Buchanan writes in his
book *Ubiquity*,

> Our human longing for explanation may be terribly misplaced, and
> doomed always to go unsatisfied. If our world is at all times tuned
> to be on the edge of sudden radical change, then [earthquakes] and
> other upheavals may all be strictly unavoidable, even just moments
> before they strike. [2000, p. 68]

This last sentence comes from a chapter called "The hinge of fate".

There are seldom simplistic explanations for the accidental: they
are not part of any grand design, as some theistic ideas may
suggest. They occur because a hundred and one chance events
come together. They are, therefore, unpredictable, and they are not
necessarily negative in their consequences, either in the short term
or the long term. Humankind lives constantly with premonition of
the accidental, which in forethought we try to prevent, but can
never assuredly control.

Chance is not quite the same as Fate—but it is our fate to live in
a world that is to some extent governed by chance, and to live daily

lives that are subject to the influence of chance, and the snowballing effect of the microscopic upon the macroscopic—whether it is the butterfly effect of chaos theory, or "for want of a nail the battle was lost". This sister Fate is a constant companion.

The third of the Fates is the most obvious fate of all—Atropos, the state of not changing, or death. Here, existentialism and Freud, although the former without too much support within psycho-analysis, converge. Both existentialism and psychoanalysis share perhaps the same roots, as Coltrera indicates:

> It is an interesting exercise in the history of ideas to note that simi-lar cultural forces at work in Germany and Austria during World War I could lead to modern existentialism on one hand, and to the basic change from the first to the second instinct theory in Freud. It is of interest, too, that the concept of death played such a great role in both developments; in modern existentialism it led to Heidegger's interest in nothingness and dread, and in Freud to the concept of the death instinct. [1962, p. 197]

Death is no accident waiting to happen, even if it sometimes comes about through an accident. It is the most significant of life's certainties. It truly is an unavoidable, unchangeable fate.

There are, then, at least these three ways of looking at the shadow cast by the Fates. Turning from theory to practice, there appear to be at least three negative responses to the idea of fate, or the individual Fates already described. There are:

1. those who dread fate—and do all in their power to try to avoid it, sometimes through obsessional ideas and behaviours;
2. those who blame fate, who see what happens to them as fate, but in doing so avoid their own part in events—with sometimes what might be called paranoid responses;
3. those who deny the significance and possibilities of fate, and live in an illusory state, as if there are no consequences to action or inaction—examples here include manic behaviours.

I concentrate upon the first two presentations as being the most likely to be seen in the consulting room. It is interesting, however, that in Sophocles' *Oedipus Rex* all three traits—avoidance, blame, and denial—are seen at different times in Oedipus himself. Most obviously, he sought to avoid fate: he ran from situations where he thought he might fulfil his fate. He was quick to blame Creon and Tiresias as plotting against him when he was confronted with his crime against the gods, and he seized upon every let-out he could before Jocasta's suicide to convince himself that he had not fulfilled the prophecy. It took her death to convince him that he had been unable to avoid his fate.

Berent (1983) presents a case of a patient who developed a facial tic as a child, in what appears to be a defence against the same fate befalling him as happened to his father. It concerns a young man whose father had been killed in a flying accident when he was 6½, which is when the tic developed. It involved throwing his eyes up towards the sky—as if when he felt most anxious he was in some way seeing the plane again.

Berent formulated the psychopathology as identification with the father as he exploded into pieces, and guarding himself from the Fates so as not to experience the same as his father. A further feature was the young man's zeal in his practice of karate, which bordered on the obsessive. Not only was he bent on becoming a karate master, with his own studio, but he also wanted to be a good street fighter. Berent describes how his patient wanted to make his body strong, his mind strong through his Master's degree as well as through therapy, and find financial security through signing up for an MBA. "Protected in body, mind, and business", writes Berent, "how could the Fates get him?" (1983, p. 289). Indeed, a phrase that his patient used was "one flicks one's finger at the Fates" (ibid., p. 293).

This appears to have been a fairly successful defence against the Fates, at least up to the point of recording the case history. A less successful example occurred in another instance that I am familiar with from a private communication. This woman had a late child-hood and adolescence that was dominated by illness; illness that she courageously faced, but one that not only left her physically scarred, but also one that prevented her from enjoying what would other-wise have been an active, fun, social life. Nevertheless, this period of her life, despite setting her back, appeared not have destroyed her love of life, her ability to get on well with others, and indeed her ability to make a fulfilling relationship, which led to a late marriage, and, late in her child-bearing years, to the birth of a son. But from this point it appears that nothing fateful was to befall her child. Despite being a capable person, she never went back to work, but devoted herself to caring for her boy. She ensured that he did all the right things, went to nursery group, went to a local school, joined in extra-curricular activities, etc. On the surface it looked as if all was going well for her child, although the observer would also have noticed that she was always at the school gate to see him off, and always there to ensure that she was present when he came out of school. She was protective of him in a way that shielded him from all difficulties—not only because he was a precious child whom she had conceived just in time—but because it appeared more and more in therapy that she wished to ensure that he never suffered as she suffered in her childhood and adolescence.

But fate cannot be avoided. It is perhaps scarcely surprising that he collapsed when it came to going away from home, getting through university, and entering the adult world with what Hamlet calls "the whips and scorns of time" (III. 1. 70). All that she had sought to protect him from appeared to descend upon him at once.

Others, as Freud observes in "The future of an illusion" seek defence from Fate in religion, although, as he says of himself and of his wish for humankind, "as for the great necessities of Fate, against which there is no help, they will learn to endure them with resignation" (1927c, p. 50).

The second attitude towards Fate is that resignation of a different kind—the denial of responsibility through blaming Fate. Introducing a case study of such a response to events, Bjerke reviews the literature on Fate, and, in common with Kaplan, finds very little reference to it in psychoanalytic articles or books. He nevertheless draws attention to Roy Schafer (1976) who approaches the psychopathology of fate from the perspective of therapeutic technique. Schafer describes interpretations in therapy as a way of re-describing, and thereby possibly modifying, a patient's unconscious "truths", so that these are no longer experienced as inevitable occurrences, as fixed fate. There seems some similarity here to cognitive–behavioural techniques such as de-catastrophizing or cognitive restructuring of irrational beliefs. Schafer uses the term "disclaiming", or denial of responsibility; and he uses it not just of some of the fixed truths that patients have, but of a great deal of traditional psychoanalytic metapsychology, which explains psychological phenomena within a mechanistic and alienating frame of reference. In Schafer's view, disclaiming is not only seen in the fate neuroses (the same term that Freud and Deutsch use), but also in cases where the patient

> defensively insists on the powerful influence of developmental deficiencies, and where he again and again describes these deficits and attributes them to constitutional factors and early irreparable traumatization caused by the environment. [Bjerke, 1995, p. 85]

The patient presents himself or herself as the victim of fate, which is seen as outside her or his control or influence. Schafer thinks it is important to analyse disclaiming, as well as excessive claiming, that is, feelings of exaggerated responsibility, including those events and experiences that are clearly outside the patient's control.

Bjerke's patient was a man who several times referred to a short story by Somerset Maugham titled "The force of circumstance" (1998). The title of the short story and some of its content were used during the therapy to highlight aspects of the patient's character, since there were a number of parallels between the story and the patient's experience. The patient used the story to support the idea "that things happened inevitably and that it was of no avail for him to intervene in his own life story" (Bjerke, 1995, p. 86).

It became clear from the patient's history, that

> external events and constellations from his earlier life were repeating themselves, seemingly unavoidably at a latter stage. Summarizing, one might say that he followed in his father's footsteps, despite his conscious wish *not* to do so. This situation gave the patient a feeling of impotence and pent-up rage. "Fate decides, it is of no avail what *I* want, it just *happens* that way." [*ibid.*, p. 87, original emphasis]

In the course of the therapy, Bjerke questioned whether the repetitions of circumstance, such as following in father's footsteps, were indeed predestined, and therefore unavoidable. Perhaps the patient's unconscious participated in choices he made; perhaps, too, there were benefits from seeing himself as a helpless victim of circumstance.

"The force of circumstance" appeared in different ways during the therapy. Bjerke comments:

Every time he had attempted to strike out a new course for himself, he experienced that he failed and inevitably ended up on a course determined by forces beyond himself. Purely biographically, there appeared to be many similarities between the analysand and the main character in the story. [*ibid.*, p. 88]

In sessions, too, the patient showed a tendency to deflect difficult topics with the phrase "anyhow, it's no use". As Bjerke writes,

Schafer's description of disclaiming (denying, depriving, relinquishing) as a characteristic defence against recognizing one's personal participation (personal agency), seems to fit in very well in this context. [*ibid.*]

The patient was eventually able to see himself as more than a victim, and more as someone who had real choices.

This is, of course, a different outcome to that which is seen in the person who seeks to control Fate; these two responses to Fate are quite opposite, and yet the more balanced attitude in each case would be an acceptance of the inevitable, whatever form it may take, together with the acceptance of responsibility when the opportunity presents itself.

Bjerke defines "fate neurosis" more clearly than earlier writers:

Fate neurosis is . . . a pattern of unpleasant, repetitive external events . . . Fate neurosis consists partly in ascribing all that happens to an unavoidable fate and partly in instigating in part dramatic and disastrous external events . . . [T]his compulsion to instigate repetitive disastrous events may furthermore lead to an experience of a more extensive, unavoidable fate ... Upbringing, religion and real external events may contribute to a consolidation of an extensive experience of fate of this kind. [*ibid.*, p. 89]

While concentrating on attitudes to Fate that can be seen in some patients, it should not be overlooked that such attitudes have relevance for therapists as well. There may be points where therapists are tempted to think that there is nothing that can be done to change what the Fates have determined. There may, in contrast, be times when therapists believe that "tragic fates can be undone, comic restoration becomes a permanent possibility, an object of practical faith" (Lear, 1996, p. 693)—this, Lear suggests, comes about through the therapeutic relationship. But not always! Freud too, in unusually optimistic mood, seems to suggest that the only way of becoming independent of Fate is "the way of life which makes love the centre of everything, which looks for all satisfaction in loving and being loved" (1930a, p. 82).

That therapists should come down on the side of "nothing can be done", or on the side of "tragic fates can be undone" is a mistaken way of looking at things. There are times when Fate must have its say. There are times when responsible choices can be made in an attempt to fly in its face. But the mistake must never be made of denying its power, however much as rational beings we prefer to demythologize the gods.

CHAPTER TEN

A maturing professional approach

T he paper that has been adapted for this chapter was published in 1990. Coming back to it after all this time, I find that
some of what I was writing in the lecture that is reproduced
in Chapter One is very much the same. Does that mean I have not
moved on? I think not, since my desire of unrest in 1990 with the
way I perceived some training for counselling and psychotherapy,
and my desire of unrest years later in that lecture are the same.
However, there were points where I felt less bold in 1990, and I
have found myself revising those in editing the paper for this book.

What interests me further about this paper is that the marks of
the mature practitioner predate a few of the definitions of how a
mature practitioner might be defined, which appeared in a summary I wrote of discussions of a BACP working party on the difference between counselling and psychotherapy. The working party
agreed that the key differences were not so much in the names
themselves, but in the quality of the practitioner, which could mean
a mature counsellor worked at a higher (deeper?) level than a new
psychotherapist. Training and supervision do make a difference, of
course, but the labels were less important than the standards of
practice (or, as we called them, the standards of excellence) that

practitioners had reached. In a short article for BACP, I concluded with the working party's definition of a mature practitioner, as someone who shows:

- an advanced level of knowledge, which includes human growth and development, psychopathology, the theory and practice of other modalities or methodologies, research methods, and awareness;
- a mature sense of judgement and confidence in decision-making in relation both to assessment and the process of therapy; the ability to conduct evaluations;
- the ability to think and focus while remaining in psychological contact with the client; to think while containing anxious situations;
- the capacity to evaluate work in progress, which includes self-evaluation, monitoring of one's own judgement, the development of an "internal supervisor";
- an attitude towards supervision which views it not simply as a requirement for training and for the oversight of her or his work, but as a valued consultancy for deepening understanding and developing practice, including knowing when to seek specific help;
- the ability to learn from errors and mistakes, through non-defensive reflection on practice—a process that increases rather than diminishes the range of clients and issues which the therapist can contain and work with;
- ongoing openness to learning including the fluid integration of knowledge into practice;
- the ability to work, and the experience of working, with a broad range of clients and contexts, including the skills of assessing the right length of contracts;
- ease with not knowing, and the ability to relinquish the need to be authoritative; together with confidence in one's competence;
- a genuine sense of humility about her or his abilities, where it is more likely to be others who recognise the excellence of the practitioner rather than the practitioner herself or himself;
- self-acceptance, a confident presence, consistent commitment, recognisable effectiveness and obvious professionalism when engaged with clients, students or supervisees;
- ongoing personal development and self-knowledge from a variety of experiences within and outwith the discipline;

- signs of increasing effectiveness with the passage of time (the length of which will vary from person to person), with the opportunities to work with an increasing number and range of clients, for the assimilation of learning, and for developing the cutting-edge of theory and practice. [Jacobs, 2001, pp. 16–17]

Little happened in response to this—perhaps the problem of the distinction between counselling and psychotherapy was dropped. Nevertheless, I believe we produced as good a set of standards as any to define what I also attempted to define in my 1990 paper as a maturing professional approach.

* * *

In his book *True and False Experience* (1973) the formerly "orthodox" psychoanalyst Peter Lomas looks at the need for psychotherapy and psychotherapists to develop beyond the necessary first steps that Freud took in his understanding both of technique and the nature of the therapeutic relationship to more emphasis on the real human relationship between therapist and patient. Peter Lomas's writing generally is refreshingly critical, and sometimes disarmingly unguarded in the clinical examples he uses. He is perhaps more optimistic than I in his belief in the capacity of inexperienced therapists to follow his lead from the very start of their practice, although my experience of novice counsellors is that they can work remarkably well, because of their enthusiasm to care, which communicates itself to the client. This can happen as long as they are not to tied down to "doing everything right".

Towards the end of the book, Lomas recounts that Winnicott suggested that no analyst should depart from recommended technique until he had ten years' experience of routine practice behind him. But Lomas puts it another way, no doubt drawing upon his own experience of the training requirements within the Institute of Psychoanalysis. He suggests that "it takes ten years for most psychoanalysts to gain the confidence to depart from a technical approach which they should never have adopted in the first place" (*ibid.*, p. 147). He has argued elsewhere (Lomas & Jacobs, 1991) that new therapists have, of course, many years of life experience upon which to draw, and that his approach, which includes being more self-disclosing than the stereotype of the analyst (although see my examples in Chapter One) is not therefore open only to those who have years of experience of the practice of psychotherapy.

Lomas is particularly critical of the blank screen type of understanding of the therapeutic relationship; he puts forward arguments for relating with clients in the positive ways in which people can do with each other. He is also critical of other inappropriate aspects of technique, and, indeed, does not like the term "technique" at all. He also makes it clear that there are ways of responding that are to be encouraged as well as ways of reacting to clients that are to be avoided, and in setting out such guidelines (such as not retaliating when clients provoke us) he lays down markers of a sort for alternative techniques. I, too, do not like the term "technique" if it stands for ways of being and responding that are rigidly learnt in training or from books (see Rowan & Jacobs, 2003) and applied in situations just because that is what has been taught in training and in books. But the repertoire of responses that can be made in particular situations, and that fit the mood of the moment, happen also to be techniques that can be learnt, more often than not from personal experience of what appears to work.

It is easier for those who are as experienced in practice as Lomas is to take a confident and critical look at concepts and practices that have become common currency for counsellors and therapists, and for them to demonstrate that they are less important than they were once thought to be. Lomas questions, for example, how important it is to stress transference today, in the way that it needed to be stressed when it was first identified. Some ideas become commonplace, he argues, startling and even shocking though they may once have been. I also find myself questioning whether transference is, in the end, as useful a term as we once thought it to be. It is clear, first, that transference is not confined to therapy, and that it is such a pervasive part of all human relationships. Second, it is familiar as a phenomenon, though less as a technical term, in common parlance, when people generally recognize in certain situations that they perceive others as "just like . . . my mother, father, teacher, ex-wife, former antagonist, boss, etc.". We might wonder in the end whether the term means anything special at all. When we look at transference more closely, it appears to denote how aspects of one's whole previous history of relating and relationships are potentially transferred into all subsequent relating and relationships. It is an explanation not just of why people behave in such inappropriate ways in some relationships, but also of the reasons why they behave appropriately too, because they have learnt and internalized all kinds of ways of relating and responding, which they are perpetually transferring into and on to new situations. In the end, it might be that transference is simply an alternative term for the conduct of all human relationships.

But to question the special use of the term "transference" is premature should I be teaching students basic skills of counselling. At that point, that is in teaching skills of listening and responding (as in Jacobs 2000b), using such a term at all might even obscure learning of other and, at the time, more important basic lessons. Transference can be a confusing and mysterious concept if it is introduced, as it often is, from examples of intensive psychotherapy, where its manifestation is usually more intense. Nevertheless, the concept dramatically helps people to make sense of their experience, especially when the influence of the past on the present is not obvious to them, however much it may be to the observer. It is still, in practice, when it disturbs relationships, an unconscious phenomenon. This applies whether we are considering trainees, clients, or relating to others in key relationships.

Lomas suggests, that transference has been "assimilated into our ordinary appreciation of life" (1973, p. 138), but the idea of a transference interpretation has not. It certainly takes skill and confidence to handle the transference and to use references to the transference with the type of delicacy that Lomas shows in his own case examples. Even if it is a key constituent of all close relationships, in the therapeutic relationship it needs to be handled with some caution. To deliberately foster the transference in order then to be able to interpret it seems manipulative. Transference can only be considered a genuine phenomenon when it arises naturally, not by suggestion.

Lomas and Winnicott and many others who are important authorities in the field of therapy and counselling are all in good company, since most of them have in some way or other chosen to break away either from the established theory or technique learnt in their own training. Indeed, such people have become authoritative partly because they have made distinctive contributions of their own. But they sometimes speak and act in therapy in ways that might puzzle the technical correctness of new counsellors and neophyte therapists.

Beginning therapists are frequently like rule-conscious children. There is nothing obsessional about this, but, like children learning the rules of new games, they insist they are stuck to, even when adults try to change them. So it is that students of counselling sometimes elevate what they have learnt to the status of inviolable technique or practice, whatever school they have been trained in. They say nothing about themselves, if trained perhaps in a psychodynamic school, even though they are longing to say "me too"; or they generate all the warmth they can, if trained perhaps in a person-centred approach, even when they do not feel it with a particular client; or they refuse to give any advice, if in one approach or another they have been taught to be non-directive. In one way, these students are right. When they started their training they had to unlearn ways of helping and relating that they thought were natural and fine, but that they were told (with good reason) were not part of a counselling approach. What was and what was not good practice was spelled out to them. And they discovered that it was indeed the case that many of the new techniques they had been taught worked rather well, and helped them to facilitate their clients in expressing themselves more fully. Their reading, too, provided fairly clear guidelines about what should and should be done (even if the "shoulds" were not printed on the page), and about what was good and bad counselling, or right and wrong technique. So, trainees have learnt that it is important to keep relatively quiet, that time boundaries should always be adhered to, that answering a client's question about yourself can be carefully side-stepped, and that touch is probably out, or in some schools of training is probably in, and that in all circumstances they need to proceed with care and caution.

And, at least in the training schemes with which I have in the past been associated, when these students have begun to get used to such basic approaches to counselling, they move on to more advanced skills and to more complex theories. In courses I once developed, they have gone on to learn about psychodynamic concepts of personality development and structure, or in their psychotherapy training they moved on to reading detailed, fully referenced articles in the journals. Or perhaps I was optimistic, because perhaps they did not read as critically as I imagined, but formed instead, on the basis of what they had been told and what they had partially read, mental pictures of the work of the most important writers, of the leading analysts and famous therapists like Klein, Winnicott, Guntrip, Fairbairn, Jung, Freud, and so on. No doubt in other orientations their students build up similar, perhaps somewhat equally idealized pictures of Rogers, Berne, Ellis, and other such figures. I make the assumption that what I have seen happening in training in my theoretical base is just as prevalent in any other orientation, since in the course of interviewing trainees for placements, from a variety of trainings, I detect something similar.

I suspect we probably build up in ourselves and in our students a mythology of how the great therapists worked. We imagine their technique to be straight down the line, perfect examples of how it should be done: gentle silence, relaxed concentration, the brilliantly timed, succinct interpretation, followed by patient working through. And our students want to be like them, and we want to be like them, and our students want to be like us. So we begin to construct what we believe to be an ideal psychotherapeutic style that our students continually seek to live up to, and, especially in those early days of training, it might be very difficult for them to re-learn how to use some of the very ways of being and relating that they have tried so hard to unlearn.

If this is so, if there is a tendency to create idealized pictures of the "big names" at work, and to elevate therapeutic techniques above more mundane interactions in therapy, this might mean that we fail to see just what a variety of approaches there are, and just how much those who have matured professionally have moved beyond theoretical and technical correctness. I suspect, when we read published case histories, which for the most part "select dramatic episodes to highlight a conclusion" (Cannon, 1974, p. 161), that we often pay more attention to the client's symptoms and phantasies, which can be extraordinarily interesting, and to brilliant interventions, than we do to the more ordinary human aspects of the therapist's manner. It might even be that the psychopathology of the client is more interesting than that of the analyst, whose main role seems, as we might presume at least from classical psychoanalytic technique, a somewhat anonymous detective unravelling the intricacies of the case.

Actually, some case histories reveal much more than we often take care to see. It is interesting to read them with the therapist in mind, and with less emphasis on the client or upon the technical aspects of the work. Indeed, we might ask, as one analyst does, "what happens in the more humdrum daily flow of analysis?" (*ibid.*). In Chapter One, I drew upon some of the accounts of those who have been patients of celebrated therapists (pp. 9–12). In addition to this, and setting apart the early analysts like Freud and Klein analysing their own children (which would now be regarded as singularly inappropriate), we know that Freud gave the patient known as the Wolf-Man food and money, and talked with him about quite casual matters (Obholzer, 1980), and there are many other hints of a far from austere psychoanalytic approach. Masud Khan writes about going on for an extra time in order to allow a patient to complete his story (1983, p. 142). Yalom invited a patient to ask him personal questions, and wrote a book with her on their therapeutic relationship (Yalom & Elkin, 1990). Robert Moody, a leading Jungian analyst, phoned one of his most vulnerable patients most nights to find out how she was, and sometimes even went round and tucked her up in bed (Ferguson, 1973). These examples might or might not come as a pleasant surprise. They are simply glimpses of the way in which those who have reached a stage of mature practice are more fully at ease with themselves, and are not hidebound by what are, in the end, technical considerations. Many of those who seem austere names on the spines of important books act in much more spontaneous ways than we would suppose from their more formal writing.

In nearly every case, it appears that these shifts away from traditional practice are made in the interests of the patient or client. Robert Moody, in being intensely nurturing, was working with a deeply regressed client. Something of that way of being is also seen in some of Winnicott's work (e.g., Little, 1990). Some analysts have drawn obvious attention to very different ways that are necessary in working with some patients. Thus Balint, in describing the phenomenon of "the basic fault" writes of two levels of analytic work. In the area of the basic fault the use of adult language, the usual verbal interchange between therapist and patient is impossible. Ordinary explanations are not understood. Balint describes it in this way:

> Common words which until then have had an agreed conventional "adult" meaning and could be used without any great conse-quence, become immensely important and powerful, either in a good or a bad sense . . . Moreover . . . the patient somehow seems able to get under the analyst's skin. [1968, p. 18]

In response to this and other indications, Balint writes that the analyst

> finds it rather difficult to maintain his usual attitude of sympa-thetic, objective passivity . . . some analysts allow, or even elect, to be carried away by this forceful current and must then change their techniques accordingly. [*ibid.*, p. 20]

Similarly, Winnicott writes of one particular patient:

> I have had to make personal growth in the course of this treatment which was painful and which I would gladly have avoided. In particular I have had to learn to examine my own technique when-ever difficulties arose. [1958, p. 280]

Balint and Winnicott are clearly aware of the need to examine and re-examine their technique. They write, of course, in the context of particularly challenging therapeutic situations, and this qualification needs to be taken seriously by those tempted to "experiment" without real cause. Yet, I would not want to confine their ability to adapt their approach to deeply disturbed clients, or to those with particular types of presenting difficulty. What Balint and Winnicott demonstrate is what Ferenczi called "the elasticity of psycho-analytic technique" (1928). Writing in a paper of that title, Ferenczi stated that "analysis should be regarded as a process of fluid development unfolding itself before our eyes rather than as a structure with a design pre-imposed upon it by an architect" (1928, p. 90).

But we do not need to look to the major writers on therapy for evidence that, as we develop in our confidence as therapists, we ourselves can begin to test out the boundaries of our training. Unfortunately, in conversations with peers, in supervision, in casework groups, or even in our written examples, we tend to draw upon what we think is expected of us by our colleagues or students. We tend to leave unsaid those moments when we bend the rules, or when we say what appears at first to be completely the wrong thing, and yet something that achieves a dramatic breakthrough for our client. And, of course, we make mistakes. In order to join the ranks of the profession, we play the game by the apparent rules of the profession—or, at least, we appear to play the game by those rules when we talk about our work to others.

I am aware that I, too, have become one of those who, less illustrious than the great names, have nevertheless become known through my writing and video work. My own technique and style has become public property. So, perhaps I can usefully submit some examples of my own, which illustrate the difference between the public persona and the private therapist. I hope that this will encourage the reader to think of examples of their own: where what you say you do differs from what you actually do, or where what you think you do in fact differs from the way your client sees what you do. (Research has shown that a therapist and a client can perceive the same session is very different ways.)

In the early 1980s, I made a video of a supervision session. One of my later supervisees told me that she was surprised when she saw the film, since it did not reflect her own experience of me. Allowing for my own development during that time, I think she was also seeing that, in supervision itself, in the confidential privacy of my own room, I would chance my arm, and express myself much more freely than I dared to do in a studio, or on a film that I knew would be carefully scrutinized by students and professionals. When we finished her period of supervision with me, and were reviewing the way we had worked together, she said, "I must tell you now that when I first told someone I wanted to see you for supervision, she said, 'Are you sure you want to see him? He really is *very* psychodynamic.' I have to say", she said, "that I haven't yet discovered what that meant."

A second example: another supervisee was very conscious of the value of remembering as much as is possible of the session; he felt this all the more strongly because he had read what I had written about the necessity for good listening. He was sometimes concerned that his memory was not up to the standard of the guidelines I had set out in *Swift to Hear*: "Listen with undivided attention, without interrupting. Remember what has been said, including the details (the more you listen and the less you say, the better your memory)" (2000b, p. 19). His inability to remember in great detail seemed to him to be a comment on his depth of listening.

Outside supervision one day, we were talking about the value of the supervisor being able to free associate to the material presented in supervision. I began to give him an example from my own experience of counselling itself, that sometimes I find myself thinking much more about what is going on in my own mind than listening to what the client is saying. But I tend not, when I realize it, to stop the client and ask him to repeat what he has said, because I have not understood it, even though this is another suggestion I make in one of my books! I keep quiet, because (this time in line with my own guidelines) I would rather not interrupt, and I would rather say no more than is necessary.

Instead of interrupting, and also instead of suddenly turning back my attention to the client, I sometimes find myself going on to reflect on what I was thinking, and what it might be telling me about the client. All this time, of course, I am continuing to miss, or, at best, I only half hear, what the client is saying. When I have done my little bit of thinking and reflection, I then probably go back to a mood of attentive listening to the client. My attention is then rather more active, because I am aware of having quite a lot to catch up on! I try to look for some clues as to what I might have missed in the client's story.

But, as I said to my supervisee, a little exaggeratedly to make the point, "I reckon that sometimes I'm listening to myself half the time, and to the client the other half of the time." "It's a relief to hear you say that," said my supervisee, "because it makes me feel better about my difficulty with remembering." My off-the-cuff remark had given him, I hope, more confidence to listen to his own inner voice, which, from the work he had already presented to me, clearly helped him reflect more deeply upon what his clients were expressing.

But then I find myself up against a dilemma. Should I go back and rewrite my books, and bring them up to date with where I am now? A new edition of a book of course gives me that opportunity, and working through my papers for this book has also allowed me to do that. But should my writing communicate to the student reader what I have taken all this time to discover, so that they can use that learning straightaway? I certainly did not hold back with the supervisee I have just described. Perhaps technique is not that sacrosanct (even though most courses of training start with it). Would it be wise to say "Listen to your client but also listen to yourself, even if you drift off into your own thoughts", in the way I myself do when I start reflecting upon the parallels between my private thoughts and my client's story? Or should we be cautious and take those at the earliest stage of their training through more straightforward guidelines?

There is some support from Lomas's argument, which says that relationships are more important than technique, for not obscuring the significance of that relationship with guidelines about how to listen and respond, but then risk turning the therapist into a machine. Janet Mattinson cites Lomas as well as Searles in support of her view that the student social worker needs to get emotionally involved in their therapeutic endeavour. She writes that, as a tutor for social work, she often said that she did not mind how involved students became, because their supervisor could always then attempt to pull them back; that it was better that they should get into a situation than maintain a distance because they were afraid of their own reactions. She comments that she was surprised how well students did with many of their clients, despite, or perhaps because, they walked into "the situation with both feet, often with a rather clumsy jump, before getting out of it" (1975, p. 41). Jumping in with both feet does not always result in the right words or actions: but if students are encouraged to be honest about everything they say to clients, they can learn from mistakes and get it right another time. The emphasis here is a little different from Lomas's: it is to get into situations, and to learn from your mistakes when you make them, rather than stand timidly on the edge, for fear of causing too big a splash. The other difference from Lomas is that while he acknowledges that a spontaneous and open psychotherapeutic approach is neither easy nor painless nor sentimental, he pays less attention to the significance of countertransference than does Mattinson.

Against these arguments, I do not forget that Winnicott was not exactly a conformist himself, and yet he advised waiting ten years before beginning to depart from recommended technique. I need to take notice of his voice of experience, too. Elsewhere, he writes of adolescence that parents need to allow young people to be immature, as long as adults do not abdicate responsibility (1971, pp. 149–150). Those words seem to support Mattinson's approach to her students, but they also remind us that maturity is reached via a phase of adolescence, where accepted wisdom might be questioned, where traditions are torn apart, where parental rules are mildly or seriously flouted, and where long tried solutions are re-examined. All this is part of development towards a more mature approach.

That there should be a period when everything is up for re-examination seems very important in training. A type of adolescent period in training needs to be recognized, and, as far as it can, to be encouraged without destroying its spontaneity, as long as responsibility for the clients in our care is not abdicated. There is nothing creative about turning out therapists and counsellors as clones, because such products will fail to recognize the uniqueness of their clients, including the unique combinations of possible reasons for their clients' difficulties. Harold Searles, writing of the termination of a supervisory relationship, draws upon the parallel of "the father's need to realize and accept that his son's individuality can never find its highest realization under the family roof" (1962, p. 604). "Effective supervision", he concludes, "helps the student to become not a carbon copy of one's professional self, but rather an individual man among men."

Such an adolescence must be preceded by a period of basic learning, of walking before we run, or learning to cycle before taking hands off the handlebars. I doubt whether it can be done before the rules and the tradition that lie behind technique and theory have been learnt and tried out in practice. We have to develop out of something, not in a vacuum. The problem with this period is that it tends towards constriction of the personality, with so much emphasis first, and rightly so, upon the needs of the client, and second, unavoidably but rather less healthily, upon the need to conform to the requirements of the training organization or professional society in order to become qualified. No wonder that students in training can complain that they are not allowed to be themselves, and that they experience a period of artificiality.

Ideally, therefore, the growing professional approach will include a more active and experimental adolescent period, which involves questioning of technique and theory, and perhaps the testing of some boundaries. Again, if this can be done while still in regular supervision, the supervisor can always help to pull back the over-zealous or over-reactive practitioner. It is certainly important that supervision should help move the counsellor or therapist into a more open approach that encourages as much personal growth in the therapist as it does in the client (Searles, 1962, pp. 584–586).

But an adolescent phase should not in itself be mistaken for maturity. It may well be marked by too much certainty, by over-simplification, by the wish to be independent of therapy and supervision, as though we can do it on our own. Lomas's 1973 book reads at times like an overstatement, sometimes with an air of certainty that might mark it out as part of an adolescent overthrowing of the established order of psychotherapy. (To do him justice, Lomas is trying to keep his argument simple in order that it may be understood; and he certainly does not believe the approach he suggests is easy.) The history of psychotherapy and counselling is, of course, full of those breakaway movements that have resulted sometimes from an authoritarian organization restricting growth, but sometimes from the impatience of psychologically adolescent therapists, who, in some of the changes they have carried out in technique, or shifts in theoretical base, have shown what appears to be unrealistic adolescent optimism for rapid solutions to the complex problems of human suffering.

It is here again that we need to look at what psychodynamic theory has termed "the countertransference". Wherein lies the motive for the change in technique? Is it in the wish of the therapist to bypass those huge barriers to progress with which we are all familiar? Or from the therapist's own wish for self-satisfaction or aggrandisement? Or does the shift in technique come from a real recognition of a different possibility for helping the client trust, learn, or change? I find myself very suspicious, for example, of Brian Thorne's example of going beyond the core conditions in his book *Person-Centred Counselling and Spirituality* (1991). While the phrase he uses for his chapter "Beyond the core conditions" is exactly in line with the type of argument I am supporting here, I am not at all sure whether the shift from a purely verbal interaction to nude massage of highly erotic parts of his client's body fully takes account of his own countertransference and her own transference. Like Lomas's work within the psychodynamic tradition, Thorne's example has given rise to considerable division of opinion in the person-centred tradition. Yet the debate is an important one.

Training organizations and professional societies also have to mature, and to pass through the various stages of childhood and adolescence on their way towards maturity. That is an even more complex area, involving as it does group processes over a long period of time. Perhaps it is somewhat simpler to address the question of how we define what a maturing *individual* professional approach might be, and how we might work towards it in training courses and counselling and psychotherapy organizations.

The first mark for a maturing professional approach is the recognition that it cannot be achieved by will-power and effort alone, and that it is certainly not through gaining paper qualifications. The maturing professional approach is characterized by a refusal to be caught up in the need for achievement and status. The wish to be mature is actually quite adolescent. Maturity involves being *unself*-conscious, which is, of course, quite different from not being self-conscious! Such Germanic terms do not fall easily upon English ears, although they posses a real value in expressing the inexpressible. The same applies to "un-knowing" (which I apply to thinking and to spirituality in Jacobs, 2000a), a far more significant feature of maturity than the acceptance of "not knowing".

"Not knowing" does, however, have its place. Part of the unself-consciousness is realizing that we do not always need to be right or correct. Like much maturity, it means recognizing just how little we actually know, without neglecting the vast amount of information available to us in the literature, as well in our own practical experience. A maturing professional approach appreciates that theories are not easily applied to individuals, but that they nevertheless present us with constant pointers that our clients might or might not choose to take up. A maturing professional approach also means accepting that we make mistakes, and that we have to learn to live with them, knowing that nearly every mistake also presents the opportunity of helping us to understand ourselves or our clients better. The acceptance of the inevitability of making mistakes also frees us for those bolder steps that begin to mark out a growing confidence in both our own and our clients' ability to push at the frontiers of self-revelation. (See some examples in Jacobs, 1992.)

Another mark of the maturing professional is the relinquishment of therapeutic ambition. Freud addresses this issue in his papers on technique:

> ... the feeling that is most dangerous to a psycho-analyst is the therapeutic ambition to achieve by this novel and much disputed method something that will have a convincing effect upon other people. This will not only put him into a state of mind which is unfavourable for his work, but will make him helpless against certain resistances of the patient whose recovery, as we know, primarily depends on the interplay of forces in him. [1912e, p. 115]

Searles puts it a different way, drawing attention to the way in which therapist and client can get "enmeshed unwittingly in making retaliatory demands on one another—the patient demands relief from suffering; and he (the therapist) demands a greater degree of self-awareness than the patient yet possesses" (1962, p. 589). Searles points out that this mutual demandingness is a defence on the part of both parties "against a growingly fond contentment with one another" (ibid.).

Winnicott, Lomas, Mattinson, and Searles agree, although they may each express it slightly differently, that we need to develop beyond technique to the centrality of the relationship between the therapist and the client. So, maturity means being able to identify with the strong feelings present in the client, by acknowledging (at least to oneself) similarly strong feelings in oneself, and thus allowing them to enter the therapeutic relationship from both sides. A mature professional approach encourages these feelings to be expressed, mainly, but not exclusively, by the client, and to be worked through without fear and shame.

Maturity also suggests a sense of growing personal integration, which may have been brought about partly through personal therapy, and partly through greater life experience. Personal therapy should, at the very least, provide the ability to develop towards that deeper reflection upon oneself that is essential in the mature therapist. One hopes that it gives therapists the confidence to engage in therapeutic relationships in a deeper and more honest way, one that does not use the client for their own ends. A mature outlook also means recognizing that personal therapy and experience does not get rid of strong feelings; it enables us to channel them in more constructive ways. We cease to be as afraid of them. In the beginning, training encourages holding back of feelings, and containing them through adherence to clear technical procedures. A maturing professional approach means allowing such feelings to gain expression *within* the therapist (although probably less rarely *between* therapist and client). Searles writes of the supervisee that

> in achieving his own potential larger self, he will on innumerable occasions need affirmation from the supervisor that the feelings he is having are "all right" for him to be having, and that his responses to the patient are "all right" too, or at any rate probably not irremediably destructive. [1962, pp. 586–587]

The significance of allowing strong countertransference feelings is, of course, not for our own pleasure or gratification, but for the deepening understanding of the current therapeutic relationship, through which the client may find some relief and possibility of change.

A mature professional approach is one that is not submerged by our own or our client's anxieties, or by the strong feelings that may be evoked in any therapeutic encounter. Rather than drown in them or being swept away by them, we learn to swim in them and with them, knowing that our ability to be immersed in the fullness of our own experience may eventually help the client to get in touch with the fullness of hers or his. Rosemary Gordon, in writing of the significance of the "I–Thou" in the therapeutic relationship, describes how she feels that more of herself is brought into the relationship as the patient's internal world becomes less stressful (1974, p. 187). But might this cause and effect might be reversed, so that the therapist's ability to bring more of himself or herself (not necessarily explicitly) into the therapeutic relationship might actually have the effect of helping make the client's internal world less stressful?

The increasing confidence of the maturing therapist in him- or herself, in the ability to handle the feelings in the therapeutic relationship, and the growing belief that it is the relationship itself which makes all the difference, perhaps helps the mature professional approach to be more flexible, and spontaneous. Greater flexibility and spontaneity in their turn inevitably give rise to the need to handle unusual feelings and situations. The willingness to do this can be distinguished from the less careful taking of risks that might be present in a more adolescent phase of professional development. The difference is that the maturing professional approach has more confidence in being able to handle the outcome, or even has some ideas as to possible outcomes, should the therapist decide to alter a boundary, to bend in some respect in relation to accepted practice, or to introduce a more personal element to the relationship than would normally be felt wise for beginning therapists. There is, in the mature approach, a greater awareness of possible consequences, and the courage to believe that the consequences will serve the good of the client in the end, even if the therapist makes, as he or she surely will, some mistakes. But perhaps the central feature of a maturing professional approach is also the central feature of therapy itself, that is the confidence, quietly but unfailingly expressed by the therapist that, whatever happens, both therapist and client, and the therapy itself, will survive.

A maturing professional approach is, thus, one that is much less clear-cut than in the earlier stages of training and practice; a different form of confidence begins to take root, confidence in the lack of certainty, and confidence in accepting the more hazy boundaries that in fact appear to exist between therapist and client. We may take some comfort from Winnicott's delightful phrase about human maturity itself: "The mature human being is neither so nice nor so nasty as the immature. The water in the glass is muddy, but not mud" (1988, p. 138).

REFERENCES

Abraham, H. C., & Freud, E. L. (Eds.) (1965). *A Psychoanalytic Dialogue: The Letters of Sigmund Freud and Karl Abraham, 1907–1926*. New York: Basic Books.

Anzieu, D. (1986). *Freud's Self-Analysis*. International Psycho-Analytic Library, 118: 1–596.

Balint, M. (1968). *The Basic Fault*. London: Tavistock.

Bass, B. M. (1960). *Leadership, Psychology and Organizational Behavior*. New York: Harper.

Berent, I. (1983). The karate master. *Annual of Psychoanalysis, 11*: 279–309.

Bettelheim, B. (1978). *The Uses of Enchantment: The Meaning and Importance of Fairy Tales*. London: Penguin.

Bettelheim, B. (1982). *Freud and Man's Soul*. London: Penguin.

Bion, W. R. (1961). *Experiences in Groups and Other Papers*. London: Tavistock.

Bion, W. R. (1967). Notes on memory and desire. *Psychoanalytic Forum, 2*: 272–273, 279–280.

Bjerke, E. (1995). Victim of fate? *Scandinavian Psychoanalytic Review, 18*: 80–90.

Bollas, C. (1989). *Forces of Destiny*. London: Free Association Press.

Brown, J. F. (1936). *Psychology and the Social Order*. New York: McGraw-Hill.

Buchanan, M. (2000). *Ubiquity*. London: Weidenfeld and Nicolson.

Byatt, A. S. (1990). *Possession*. London: Chatto and Windus.

Cannon, A. (1974). Transference as creative illusion. In: M. Fordham, R. Gordon, J. Hubback, & K. Lambert (Eds.), *Technique in Jungian Analysis*. London: Heinemann Medical.

Capps, D. (1983). *Life Cycle Theory and Pastoral Care*. Fortress Press.

Cartwright, A. (1996). Psychoanalytic self psychology. In: M. Jacobs (Ed.), *In Search of Supervision* (pp. 36–52). Buckingham: Open University Press.

Cell, C. P. (1974). Charismatic heads of state: the social context. *Behavior Science Research*, 9: 255–305.

Coltrera, J. T. (1962). Psychoanalysis and existentialism. *Journal of American Psychoanalytic Association*, 10: 166–215.

Conrad, J. (1963). *The Nigger of the Narcissus*. London: Penguin.

Couch, A. S. (1995). Anna Freud's adult psychoanalytic technique: a defence of classical analysis. *International Journal of Psycho-Analysis*, 76(1): 153–171.

de Maistre, J. (1851). *Lettres et oposcules inédits*. Paris: A. Valcon.

Deri, F., & Brunswick, D. (1964). Freud's Letters to Ernst Simmel. *Journal of the American Psychoanalytic Association*, 12: 93–109.

Deutsch, H. (1930). Hysterical fate neurosis. In: H. Deutsch, *Neuroses and Character Types—Clinical Psychoanalytic Studies* (pp. 14–28). New York: International Universities Press, 1965.

Dryden, J. (1985). *Poems and Prose*. London: Penguin Poetry Library.

Durham, M. S. (1990). The therapist and the concept of revenge: the law of talion. *The Journal of Pastoral Care*, 44: 2.

Eco, U. (1983). *The Name of the Rose*. London: Secker and Warburg.

Ellis, A. (1967). Rational–emotive psychotherapy. In: D. S. Arbuckle (Ed.), *Counseling and Psychotherapy*. New York: McGraw Hill.

Erikson, E. (1964). *Childhood and Society*. London: Penguin.

Farrell, M. (1994). J'accuse: the revenge theme in the lawyer's world. Unpublished paper.

Ferenczi, S. (1928). The elasticity of psycho-analytic technique. In: M. Balint (Ed.), *Final Contributions to the Problems and Methods of Psycho-Analysis* (pp. 87–101). New York: Basic Books, 1955.

Ferguson, S. (1973). *A Guard Within*. London: Penguin.

Freud, A. (1965). *Normality and Pathology in Childhood*. London: Hogarth.

Freud, S. (1895d). *Studies on Hysteria*. S.E., 2. London: Hogarth.

Freud, S. (1900a). *The Interpretation of Dreams*. S.E., 4. London: Hogarth.

Freud, S. (1905a). *Three Essays on Sexuality*. S.E., 7. London: Hogarth.

Freud, S. (1907b). Obsessive actions and religious practices. *S.E.*, *9*.: 115–128. London: Hogarth.

Freud, S. (1908d). "Civilized" sexual morality and modern nervousness. *S.E.*, *9*: 177–204. London: Hogarth.

Freud, S. (1909d). *Notes upon a Case of Obsessional Neurosis. S.E.*, *10*: 153–318. London: Hogarth.

Freud, S. (1911b). Formulation on the two principles of mental functioning. *S.E.*, *12*: 213–226. London: Hogarth.

Freud, S. (1911–1915). Papers on technique. *S.E.*, *12*: 85–174. London: Hogarth.

Freud, S. (1912e). Recommendations to physicians practising psychoanalysis. *S.E.*, *12*: 109–120. London: Hogarth.

Freud, S. (1913c). On beginning the treatment. *S.E.*, *12*: 121–143. London: Hogarth.

Freud, S. (1913f). The theme of the three caskets. *S.E.*, *12*: 289–302. London: Hogarth.

Freud, S. (1913i). The disposition to obsessional neurosis. *S.E.*, *12*: 311–326. London: Hogarth.

Freud, S. (1916d). Some character-types met with in psychoanalytic work. *S.E.*, *14*: 309–334. London: Hogarth.

Freud, S. (1919a). Lines of advance in psychoanalytic therapy. *S.E.*, *17*: 157–168. London: Hogarth.

Freud, S. (1921c). *Group Psychology and the Analysis of the Ego. S.E.*, *28*. London: Hogarth.

Freud, S. (1923a). Two encyclopaedia articles. *S.E.*, *18*: 233–260. London: Hogarth.

Freud, S. (1923b). *The Ego and the Id. S.E.*, *19*. London: Hogarth.

Freud, S. (1925i). Some additional notes upon dream-interpretation as a whole. *S.E.*, *19*: 125–140. London: Hogarth.

Freud, S. (1927a). Postscript to *The Question of Lay Analysis. S.E.*, *20*: 251–258. London: Hogarth.

Freud, S. (1927c). The future of an illusion. *S.E.*, *21*: 3–58. London: Hogarth.

Freud, S. (1930a). *Civilization and Its Discontents. S.E.*, *21*. London: Hogarth.

Freud, S. (1933a). *New Introductory Lectures on Psycho-Analysis. S.E.*, *22*. London: Hogarth.

Freud, S. (1933b). Why war? In: *Collected Papers*, Volume 5. London: Hogarth.

Freud, S. (1937c). Analysis terminable and interminable. *S.E.*, *23*: 209–254. London: Hogarth Press.

Freud, S. (1937d). Constructions in analysis. *S.E.*, *23*: 255–270. London: Hogarth.

Freud, S. (1939a). *Moses and Monotheism. S.E.*, *23*. London: Hogarth.

Fromm, E. (1964). *The Dogma of Christ*. London, Routledge and Kegan Paul.

Fromm, E. (1967). *Psychoanalysis and Religion*. Yale, CT: Yale University Press.

Fromm, E. (1977). *The Anatomy of Human Destructiveness*. London: Penguin.

Gay, P. (1989). *Freud: a Life For Our Time*. London: Macmillan.

Goetz, B. (1975). That is all I have to say about Freud: Bruno Goetz's reminiscences of Sigmund Freud. *International Review of Psycho-Analysis*, *2*, 139–143.

Gordon, R. (1974). Transference as the fulcrum of analysis. In: M. Fordham, R. Gordon, J. Hubback, & K. Lambert (Eds.), *Technique in Jungian Analysis*. London: Heinemann Medical.

Gouldner, A. E. (Ed.) (1965). *Studies in Leadership*. New York: Russell and Russell.

Guggenbuhl-Craig, A. (1971). *Power in the Helping Professions*. New York: Spring.

Guntrip, H. (1961). *Personality Structure and Human Interaction*. London: Hogarth.

Guntrip, H. J. S. (1996). My experience of analysis with Fairbairn and Winnicott. *International Journal of Psycho-Analysis*, *77*: 739–754.

Hardy, T. (1979). *Poems*. London: The Folio Society.

Hill, J. (1993). Am I a Kleinian? Is anyone? *British Journal of Psychotherapy*, *9*(4): 463–475.

Holbrook, D. (1971). *Human Hope and the Death Instinct*. Oxford: Pergamon.

Hollander, E. P. (1964). *Leaders. Groups and Influence*. New York: Oxford University Press.

Horney, K. (1948). The value of vindictiveness. In: H. Kelman (Ed.) (1965) *New Perspectives in Psychoanalysis; Contributions to Karen Horney's Holistic Approach*. New York: W. W. Norton.

Jacobs, M. (1987). Our desire of unrest. *The Modern Churchman*, *29*(1): 15–22.

Jacobs, M. (1992). Hard-earned lessons in counselling in action. In: W. Dryden (Ed.), *Hard-earned Lessons from Counselling in Action* (pp. 58–68). London: Sage.

Jacobs, M. (2000a). *Illusion: a Psychodynamic Interpretation of Thinking and Belief*. London: Whurr.

Jacobs, M. (2000b). *Swift to Hear* (2nd, revised, edn). London: SPCK.

Jacobs, M. (2001). Standards of excellence. *Counselling and Psychotherapy Journal, 12*: 6: 16–17.

Jacobs, M. (2006). *The Presenting Past: the Core of Psychodynamic Counselling and Therapy* (3rd edn). Maidenhead: Open University Press.

Jacoby, S. (1983). *Wild Justice: the Evolution of Revenge.* New York: Harper and Row.

Jelliffe, S. E. (1933). Address—glimpses of a Freudian odyssey. *Psychoanalytic Quarterly, 2*: 318–329.

Jennings, H. H. (1942). *Leadership and Isolation: a Study of Personality and Interpersonal Relations.* New York: Longmans, Green.

Jeremias, J. (1966). *Rediscovering the Parables.* London: SCM.

Jones, E. (1964). *The Life and Work of Sigmund Freud.* London: Penguin.

Jones, R. (1989). Supervision: a choice between equals? *British Journal of Psychotherapy, 5*: 505–511.

Jung, C. G. (1918). Preface to the second edition. *On the Psychology of the Unconscious. C.W., 7.* London: Routledge and Kegan Paul

Jung, C. G. (1935). *Relations between the Ego and the Unconscious. CW, 7.* London: Routledge and Kegan Paul.

Kaplan, D. M. (1984). Reflections on the idea of personal fate and its psychopathology: Helene Deutsch's "Hysterical Fate Neurosis" revisited. *Psychoanalytic Quarterly, 53*: 240–266.

Keiser, S. (1956). Panel report: The technique of supervised analysis. *Journal of the American Psychoanalytic Association, 4*: 539–549.

Kernberg, O. (1975). *Borderline Conditions and Pathological Narcissism.* New York: Jason Aronson.

Khan, M. (1974). *The Privacy of the Self.* New York: International Universities Press.

Khan, M. (1983). *Our Hidden Selves.* London: Hogarth.

Kidd, M. (undated). Private communication.

Klein, J. (1987). *Our Need for Others and Its Roots in Infancy.* London: Tavistock.

Klein, M. (1988). *Love, Guilt and Reparation and Other Works 1921–1945.* London: Virago.

Kohut, H. (1971). Narcissism and narcissistic rage. *The Psychoanalytic Study of the Child, 27*: 360–400.

Kovel, J. (1978). *A Complete Guide to Therapy.* London: Penguin.

Lacan, J. (1949). Le stade du miroir comme formateur de la fonction du je, telle qu'elle nous est révélée dans l'expérience psychanalytique. In: *Écrits* (1966). Paris: Éditions du Seuil.

Lacan, J. (1977). *The Four Fundamental Concepts of Psychoanalysis*. London: Hogarth.

Lampl-de Groot, J. (1976). Personal experiences with psychoanalytical technique and theory during the last half century. *Psychoanalytic Study of the Child*, 31: 283–296.

Langs, R. (1979). *The Supervisory Experience*. New York: Jason Aronson.

Lawrence, D. H. (1960). *Selected Poems*. London: Penguin.

Lear, J. (1996). The introduction of Eros: reflections on the work of Hans Loewald. *Journal of American Psychoanalytic Association*, 44: 673–698.

Le Guin, U. (1971). *A Wizard of Earthsea*. London: Puffin.

Lipton, S. D. (1979). An Addendum to "The advantages of Freud's technique as shown in his analysis of the Rat Man. *International Journal of Psycho-Analysis*, 60: 215–216.

Little, M. I. (1990). *Psychotic Anxieties and Containment: a Personal Record of an Analysis with Winnicott*. New York: Jason Aronson.

Lomas, P. (1973). *True and False Experience*. London: Allen Lane.

Lomas, P., & Jacobs, M. (1991). *In Conversation with Peter Lomas*. Videotape available from the Audio-Services Department, Medical Sciences Building, University of Leicester.

McDougall, J. (1989). *Theatre of the Body: Psychoanalytic Approach to Psychosomatic Illness*. London: Free Association.

McEwan, I. (2005). *Saturday*. London: Jonathan Cape.

Maitland, S. (1988). *A Book of Spells*. London: Methuen.

Maizels, N. (1985). Self-envy, the womb and the nature of goodness - a reappraisal of the death instinct. *International Journal of Psycho-Analysis*, 66: 185–192.

Maslow, A. H. (1987). *Motivation and Personality* (3rd edn). New York: Harper and Row.

Masson, J. (1985). *The Complete Letters of Sigmund Freud to Wilhelm Fliess 1887–1904*. Cambridge, MA: Belknap Press.

Mattinson, J. (1975). *The Reflection Process in Casework Supervision*. London: Tavistock.

Maugham, S. (1988). *Collected Short Stories*, Volume 2. London: The Folio Society.

Mearns, D., & Thorne, B. (2000). *Person-centred Therapy Today*. London: Sage.

Meng, H., & Freud, E. (Eds.) (1963). *Psychoanalysis and Faith: the Letters of Sigmund Freud and Oscar Pfister*. New York: Basic Books.

Merton, R. K. (1968). The Matthew effect in science. *Science*, 159: 59–63.

Metz, C. (1982). *Psychoanalysis and Cinema: The Imaginary Signifier*. London: Macmillan.

Murdoch, I. (1978). *The Sea, The Sea.* London: Chatto and Windus.

Obholzer, K. (1980). *The Wolf-Man.* London: Routledge and Kegan Paul.

Patton, J. (1987). *Is Human Forgiveness Possible?* Nashville, TN: Abingdon.

Prentky, R. A. (1980). *Creativity and Psychopathology.* New York: Praeger.

Racker, H. (1968). *Transference and Counter-transference.* London: Hogarth Press.

Rangell, L. (1954). Similarities and differences between psychoanalysis and dynamic psychotherapy. *Journal of the American Psychoanalytic Association, 2:* 734–744.

Redl, F. (1942). Group emotion and leadership. *Psychiatry, 5:* 573–596.

Rieff, P. (1973). *The Triumph of the Therapeutic.* London: Penguin.

Roazen, P. (1979). *Freud and His Followers.* London: Penguin.

Roe, A. (1952). A psychologist examines 64 eminent scientists. *Scientific American, 187:* 21–25.

Rogers, C. (1967). The necessary and sufficient conditions of therapeutic personality change. *Journal of Consultative Psychology, 21.*

Rogers, C. (1974). *On Becoming a Person.* London: Constable

Roudinesco, E. (1990). *Jacques Lacan & Co.: A History of Psychoanalysis in France 1925–1985.* London: Free Association.

Rowan, J. (2005). *The Future of Training in Psychotherapy and Counselling.* Hove: Routledge.

Rowan, J., & Jacobs, M. (2003). *The Therapist's Use of Self.* Buckingham: Open University Press.

Rushdie, S. (1990). *Haroun and the Sea of Stories.* London: Granta.

Rustin, M., & Rustin, M. (1987). *Narratives of Love and Loss: Studies in Modern Children's Fiction.* London: Verso.

Rycroft, C. (1968). *Psychoanalysis Observed.* London: Penguin.

Rycroft, C. (1985). *Psychoanalysis and Beyond.* London: Chatto and Windus/Hogarth.

Schafer, R. (1976). *A New Language for Psychoanalysis.* New Haven, CT: Yale University Press.

Schiffer, I. (1973). *Charisma: a Psychoanalytic Look at Mass Society.* Toronto: University of Toronto Press.

Searles, H. (1955). The informational value of the supervisor's emotional experiences. In: H. Searles, *Collected Papers on Schizophrenia and Related Subjects* (pp. 157–176). London: Hogarth, 1965.

Searles, H. (1956). The psychodynamics of vengefulness. In: H. Searles, *Collected Papers on Schizophrenia and Related Subjects* (pp. 177–191). London: Karnac, 1965.

Searles, H. (1959). Oedipal love in the counter-transference. In: H. Searles, *Collected Papers on Schizophrenia and Related Subjects* (pp. 284–303). London: Hogarth, 1965.

Searles, H. (1962). Problems of psycho-analytic supervision. In: H. Searles (1965) *Collected Papers on Schizophrenia and Related Subjects* (pp. 584–604). London: Karnac.

Searles, H. (1965). *Collected Papers on Schizophrenia and Related Subjects*. London: Hogarth/Karnac.

Sendak, M. (1970). *Where the Wild Things Are*. London: Puffin.

Simonton, D. K. (1984). *Genius, Creativity and Leadership*. Cambridge, MA: Harvard University Press.

Spengemann, W. C. (1992). Columbus and history. *Folio Society Magazine*, Spring.

Spinelli, E., & Marshall, S. (Eds.), (2001). *Embodied Theories*. London: Continuum.

Suttie, I. (1963).*The Origins of Love and Hate*. London: Penguin.

Thorne, B. (1991). *Person-Centred Counselling and Spirituality*. London: Whurr.

Tolkien, J. R. R. (1964). *Tree and Leaf*. London: Unwin.

Wallon, H. (1931). Comment se développe chez l'enfant la notion de corps proper. *Journal de Psychologie*, 705–748.

Weatherhead, L. D. (1963). *Psychology Religion and Healing* (2nd edn). London: Hodder and Stoughton.

Weinstein, F. (1980). The social function of intellectuals. In: M. Albin (Ed.), *New Directions in Psychohistory* (pp. 3–20). Washington, DC: Lexington.

Wilber, K. (2000). *Integral Psychology*. Boston, MA: Shambhala.

Wilbur, G. B., & Muensterberger, W. (Eds.) (1951). *Psychoanalysis and Culture*. New York: International Universities Press.

Winnicott, D. W. (1958). Metapsychological and clinical aspects of regression within the psycho-analytical set-up. In: *Collected Papers: from Paediatrics to Psycho-analysis*. London: Tavistock.

Winnicott, D. W. (1965). *The Maturational Processes and the Facilitating Environment*. London: Karnac.

Winnicott, D. W. (1971). *Playing and Reality*. London: Tavistock/Routledge.

Winnicott, D. W. (1988). *Human Nature*. London: Free Association.

Yalom, I. (1991). *Love's Executioner and Other Tales of Psychotherapy*. London: Penguin.

Yalom, I., & Elkin, G. (1990). *Every Day Gets a Little Closer: a Twice Told Therapy*. New York: Basic Books.

Yariv, G. (1993). Gazing into Medusa's eyes: the fear of being seen and attacks on insight. *British Journal of Psychotherapy, 10*(2): 142–158.

Zinkin, L. (1988). The impossible profession. In: *Clinical Supervision: Issues and Techniques* (pp. 15–24). Jungian Training Committee of the British Association of Psychotherapists.

INDEX